授業をグーンと
楽しくする
英語教材シリーズ
49

Small Talkで使える！

トピック別
中学生のための
すらすら英会話

瀧沢広人 著

明治図書

はじめに

　みなさん，こんにちは。岐阜大学の瀧沢広人です。小学校に外国語が導入され，教科となり，日本の英語教育の流れは大きく変化してきました。今まで不可能であったことが可能になりつつあります。そのような中，これからの中学校の英語授業づくりにおいて，ぜひ行ってほしい活動，チャレンジしてほしい活動に Small Talk があります。

　Small Talk とは，授業開始時にテーマが与えられ，そのテーマについて，生徒同士で，英語で話す活動になります。誰の支えもなく，自分たちで対話をつなげていく活動です。これこそが，生徒が育った姿の１つだと考えるのです。英語で話す生徒の姿は教師の指導の成果の現れと言えるでしょう。教師の指導が素晴らしくとも，生徒に英語力が育たなければ意味がありません。その絶好の場面が Small Talk だと考えるのです。だから研究授業があると，私は，耳をそば立て，生徒の Small Talk の様子を観察し，生徒の発話を聞くようにしています。

　試しに，生徒同士で Small Talk をさせてみます。すると，生徒の発話状況から課題が見えてきます。例えば，「相づちが打てていないな」「会話が発展していかないな」「ただ答えるだけで，詳しく話そうとしていないな」等です。そうしたら，それらの課題を１つ１つ克服するよう指導を重ねていけばいいのです。

　課題の克服には一定期間を必要とします。しかしその間，課題の克服という目標に向かって，集中的に指導していきます。すると，ある程度は，課題を克服していきます。しかし，さらに次の課題が見えてきます。そうしたら，また，その課題に向けて指導していきます。このように，指導と評価を一体化させながら，生徒の発話力を高めていくようにします。

　もし私が，今でも中学校教員であったならば，英語授業の目標の１つに，「Small Talk のできる生徒」を入れていたことと思います。

　実は，生徒は，小学校の外国語授業において Small Talk を経験してきます。私が岐阜大学へ赴任した年，小学校の授業を参観する機会がありました。驚きました。小学５年生が，ペアになって，英語で話をしているのです。私が中学校でやろうとしていたことを，小学生がやっているのです。小学生ですから，使用する語彙や表現は限られていますが，話すことに抵抗はありません。そのような児童が中学校にやって来る時代なのです。

　本書は，ぜひ，中学校で Small Talk を徹底的に行い，意図的・計画的な指導が可能となるよう，指導のヒントを提示できればという願いで執筆しました。

　なお，各学年で15のトピックを提示し，さらにその応用・発展トピックも参考として載せています。もちろん，中学３年生でも，中学１年生や２年生のトピックを使うことも可能です。多くのトピックを用い，生徒の発話力が高まることを願っています。

　さて，Small Talk には，一定の型があります。次が主な流れです。これで10分間の活動です。

①教師の Teacher's Talk
②生徒同士の Small Talk（1回目）
③中間評価
④生徒同士の Small Talk（2回目）

　そして，Small Talk 活動を通じ，目標や課題を持たせ，次のようなことを生徒に指導していきます。

◎対話を継続していく力

　対話を継続していくためには，「繰り返し」や「相づち」「質問」「感想」など，相手の発話に対して反応することを育てていきます。これも一朝一夕にはいきませんので，教師の粘り強い指導が重要です。

　また，話題を深めたり，広げたりする力も必要です。話題を深めたり，広げたりする力は，コミュニケーションを円滑に行うためにも，大事な技量となります。場合によっては，何もないところから話題を作り，場の雰囲気をよくする人もいます。沈黙が生まれたら，その沈黙を埋めるよう，話題を膨らませたりする人もいます。それもコミュニケーション能力だと考えるのです。生徒もまた，そのように育ってほしいと思います。

◎内容を整理して話す力

　いわゆる即興的な発表になります。その場で，テーマについて，順を追って話ができる生徒を育てたいと思います。「How was your summer vacation?（夏休みどうだった？）」と尋ねられ，いきなり，I went to … ではなく，総括して，どんな夏休みだったか，最初に言える生徒です。例えば，It was great. の1文でもいいですし，I enjoyed it a lot. と，トピックを表す1文を言ってから，その理由を話していくようなことも指導したいです。

　元々，Small Talk は，ビジネスの世界において，商談を行う前の人間関係づくりにあります。雑談を交わしながら，お互いをよく知り，その後の仕事の話がうまくいくようにするものであると言います。教室における Small Talk も，ゆくゆくは，授業が始まり，学習しやすい環境とするために，近くの生徒と英語で会話をし，その後の学習において，協働的に学習したり，気軽にわからないことを尋ね合ったりすることのできる Warming-up の役割となっていくべきだと考えます。

　授業冒頭の10分の活動になりますが，生徒の会話力を高め，英語学習への雰囲気を創り，学習意欲につながる Small Talk が展開されることを願っています。

2024年7月　　　　　　　　　　　　　　　　　　　　　　　　　　　　　瀧沢広人

Contents
目 次

はじめに 2

Chapter 1
授業はじめのたった10分！
簡単 Small Talk 版「すらすら英会話」の使い方 7

1 生徒の話す力を向上させる！
Small Talk の進め方 8
① Small Talk の基本形 8
② Small Talk をこんな風に取り組んでみたら？ 14
③ Small Talk の評価 16

2 Small Talk に役立つ！
「すらすら英会話」のやり方 18
① Small Talk 版「すらすら英会話」の活用法 18
② Small Talk 版「すらすら英会話」の進め方 18

コラム Small Talk のパフォーマンス評価 22

Chapter 2
中学1年で扱いたい！
トピック別「すらすら英会話」15 23

| 文法事項 | 主な表現 | 実施時期 | 留意点 | 応用・発展 |

Teacher's Talk

1【接続期①】 自己紹介　Get to know each other 24
2【接続期②】 果物や野菜　Fruit or Vegetable 26
3【接続期③】 あなたの1日　My Daily Life 28
4【接続期④】 小学校の思い出　School Memories 30
5【接続期⑤】 将来の夢　Dreams for the Future 32
6 部活動は何部？　趣味は？　Club Activity or Hobbies 34

7 ペットは何か飼っているの？　My Pet 36

8 好きな食べ物は何？　Favorite Dish 38

9 夏休みは何したい？　Plans for My Summer Vacation 40

10 夏休みの思い出　Memories of Summer Vacation 42

11 友だちや先生について教えて！　Friends or Teachers 44

12 どんな音楽を聴く？　Music 46

13 好きなことは何？　Favorite Thing to Do 48

14 冬休みの出来事　My Winter Vacation 50

15 昨夜6時頃，何していた？　Last Night 52

ひとくち英語❶　1 → 30 54

Chapter
3 中学2年で扱いたい！ トピック別「すらすら英会話」15 55

文法事項　主な表現　実施時期　留意点　応用・発展
Teacher's Talk

1 お互いを知ろう①　Get to know each other 56

2 ゴールデンウィークには何する？　Your Plans for Golden Week 58

3 ゴールデンウィークはどう過ごした？　Memories of Golden Week 60

4 お気に入りのレストランは？　My Favorite Restaurant 62

5 今夜の予定は？　Plans for Tonight 64

6 夏祭りには行くの？　Summer Festival 66

7 私たちの町はどんな町？　Our Town 68

8 お気に入りのテレビ番組は？　My Favorite TV Program 70

9 お気に入りの遊園地は？　My Favorite Amusement Park 72

10 最近どう？　What's new? 74

11 好きな季節はいつ？　Season 76

12 クリスマスはどう過ごすの？　Christmas 78

13 日本地理，どのくらい知っている？　Geography of Japan 80

14 どの教科が好き？　School Subjects 82

15 私の好きなこと　My Favorite Things 84

ひとくち英語❷　31 → 60 86

5

Chapter 4 中学3年で扱いたい！トピック別「すらすら英会話」15 ……87

| 文法事項 | 主な表現 | 実施時期 | 留意点 | 応用・発展 |

Teacher's Talk

1 お互いを知ろう② Get to know each other …… 88
2 星座は何座？ The Zodiac Sign …… 90
3 修学旅行はどこに行くの？ School Trip …… 92
4 どんな料理を作る？ Cooking …… 94
5 修学旅行はどうだった？ How was your school trip? …… 96
6 都会がいい？ 田舎がいい？ City or Countryside …… 98
7 次の目標は？ What's your next goal? …… 100
8 どんな本を読んでいる？ Reading a Book …… 102
9 あなたの夢は？ Dreams for the Future …… 104
10 あなたの好きな言葉は？ Favorite Word or Phrase …… 106
11 今年の漢字は？ What's your *kanji* of the year? …… 108
12 今年の夢は？ Dreams for This Year …… 110
13 100万円あったらどうする？ If you had one million yen, ... …… 112
14 英語と私 English and I …… 114
15 中学校の思い出は？ Memories of Junior High School …… 116
  ひとくち英語❸ 61 → 90 …… 118

Chapter 1

授業はじめのたった10分！
 Small Talk版
「すらすら英会話」
の使い方

1　生徒の話す力を向上させる！Small Talk の進め方

① Small Talk の基本形

　授業冒頭で行う Small Talk は，既習事項の定着を図り，会話を継続していく力を育てることをねらいとして行う活動です。次のような 4 つの指導手順を踏みます。

指導手順

1　教師の Teacher's Talk

❶教師が自分のことを語る。（1 分）

　Small Talk は，まず，教師の自己開示から始まります。例えば，Breakfast がテーマであれば，朝食の写真を撮っておき，それを生徒に見せながら，朝食のことを話題にします。

T : Hello, what did you eat for breakfast this morning? This is my breakfast this
　 morning. I always eat rice and *miso* soup. I usually eat *natto*, but this morning,
　 I ate grilled salmon. I like it. I also like raw eggs. So, this is my breakfast.

　教師が自己開示し，自分のことを語ると，生徒も自己を語ろうとします。まずは，教師が自分のことを話し，その上で，生徒に尋ねるようにします。この順番は逆にしないようにしたいです。

❷生徒に質問を投げかけ，英語の運用能力を確認する。（2 分）

　教師の話が終わると，今度は，生徒がどんな朝食を食べているのか知りたくなるのではないでしょうか。知りたいという気持ちは，コミュニケーションの始まりです。その素直な気持ちを表に出し，生徒と英語でやり取りをします。

T : So, this is my breakfast. What did you eat for breakfast this morning?
S1: I ate ... rice, *miso* soup, ... and salad ..., fish.
T : Grilled fish?
S1: Yes. Grilled fish.
T : Great. （grilled fish と板書）You ate grilled fish. How about you, S2?
　 What did you eat for breakfast this morning?
S2: I ate bread. （bread と板書）

8

T : Only bread?

S2: Egg.（bread の下に，egg と板書）

T : Sunny-side up?

S2: Sunny …?

T : Yes.（簡単に絵を描く）Sunny … side … up. It looks like the sun, so it is called 'Sunny-side up.'（sunny-side up と板書）

Ss: 目玉焼き！

T : Right. Did you eat your eggs sunny-side up?

S2: No. ゆで玉子.

T : How do you say 'ゆで玉子?'

S3: Boiled egg.

T : Good! ゆで玉子 is a boiled egg.（boiled egg と板書）You ate a boiled egg.

S2: Yes.

T : What else did you eat? Only bread and a boiled egg?

S2: Salad.

T : What did you eat?

S2: Cabbage and broccoli.

T : Nice. It's healthy.（healthy と板書）

O.K. Today's topic is "Breakfast." Make pairs.

このように，生徒に質問を投げかけ，その返答を利用しながら，その後の生徒同士でのSmall Talk で使用するような表現や文法事項等をさりげなく聞かせ，既習事項を思い出させます。

> **留意点**
>
> 　生徒と英語で意思疎通が図れるようになるということは，それだけで英語授業の目的が果たせたと言っても過言ではありません。昔は，英文の台本なしに英語で対話することは，なかなかできませんでした。しかし，今では，小学校に英語の授業が入ったおかげで，可能になったと感じます。Small Talk のやり取りの中でも，徐々に，「答えたら1文足してみよう」「先生にも質問してみよう」と促し，うまく言えない時には，教師が言い直してあげたり，新しい表現を教えたりしながら，生徒の語彙や表現の定着を図り，徐々に流暢な会話ができることを目指していけるとよいでしょう。個人差はありますが，意図的な指導の継続が必要だと考えます。

2 生徒同士の Small Talk（1回目）

❶テーマを提示し，ペアにさせる。（1分）

　教師の Teacher's Talk が終わったら，生徒同士の Small Talk に入ります。Small Talk の時間的な目標を，例えば，中学1年生で1分間，中学2年生で2分間，中学3年生で3分間と設定します。もちろん，中学1年生の3学期末で1分間ですので，1学期は30秒でも構いません。「できた」という成功体験を積み上げながら，段階的に話す時間を延ばします。

T : O.K. Today's topic is 'Breakfast.' Make pairs.

Ss:（隣の人と席を向かい合わせ，ペアになる）

T : I'll give you one minute. Talk about 'Breakfast.' Let's start.

　この時，大事にしたいことは，最初に必ず挨拶から始めさせることです。いきなり，What did you eat …? と入るのではなく，挨拶から始めさせるようにしましょう。

❷ Small Talk の1回目を始める。（1分）

S1: Hello. How are you?

S2: I'm good. How are you?

S1: Good, but I'm a little sleepy.

S2: Why?

S1: After lunch, I always get sleepy. How about you? Are you sleepy?

S2: No. I'm good.
　　What did you eat for breakfast this morning?

S1: I ate rice, egg, 玉子焼き, *miso* soup and some salad. How about you?

S2: I ate bread, soup, salad and yogurt.

S1: Wow, it's very healthy. What vegetables did you eat?

S2: I ate lettuce, tomato, and cucumber.

S1: Do you eat bread every morning?

S2: Yes, I always eat bread for breakfast.

〈ベルが鳴る〉

S1: Thanks for talking with me.

S2: Thank you. I enjoyed talking with you.

> **留意点**　　ベルが鳴り終わった後，お礼を述べたり，相手のことを知って，感想を述べたりするなど，終わり方を，学年ごとに目標を設定し，指導を行っていくとよいでしょう。もし，道端で外国人と出会ったら，別れ際に気の利いた一言でも発せられる生徒に育てたいと思います。
>
> 　ペアでの Small Talk の様子を見る際，教師は事前に評価ポイントを決めておきます。例えば，「アイコンタクト」や「ジェスチャー」などの非言語コミュニケーション能力の状況や，「相手のことを深く知るために質問をしている」「必要な情報を相手に詳しく伝えようとしている」等の観察ポイントを決めておき，次の中間評価に入ります。

3　中間評価（4分）

　生徒同士の Small Talk の1回目が終わると，中間評価をします。ねらいは，「よりよく会話ができるよう指導すること」です。例えば，「言いたかったけど，言えなかった表現」があった場合，それを言えるようにして，2回目の Small Talk に移ったり，「コミュニケーションに向かう態度の指導」を行ったりすることです。なお，中間評価の方法は1通りでなく，様々なやり方がありますので，色々な方法を試してみるとよいでしょう。

　中間評価の方法①　「言いたかったけど，言えなかった表現」を共有する。

　Small Talk 中に，「言いたかったけど，言えなかった表現」をクラスで共有し，他の言い方で言えないかどうか挑戦させたり，ALT に確認したり，また各自で調べさせたりします。そして，それを用い，次の Small Talk に活かすことをします。

T: 何か言いたかったけど，言えなかったことってありますか。

S1:「煮物」って，何て言うのかわかりませんでした。

T:「煮物」って，何と言うんだろう。

S2: boiled vegetable

　　（ALT がいれば，ALT に向かって通じるか確認する）

T: Boiled vegetable?

ALT: Oh, it's simmered vegetable.

T:（板書する）simmered vegetable

　中間評価の方法②　ペアで，Small Talk を振り返る。

中間評価の方法①の「言いたかったけど，言えなかった表現」をペアで行い，「私はさっき，

こう言いたかったんだけど」「こういう意味だったんだ」などの振り返りをさせます。その中で，「こう言えばよかった」「こんな風に言うといいかも」というようなことをアドバイスし合い，ペアで話し合います。わからない表現は，辞書やネットで調べさせてもよいでしょう。

T：では，ペアで，「Small Talk では，こんなことを言いたかったけど，言えなかった」「こういうことを言いたかったんだ」ということを振り返ってみましょう。そして，その「言いたかったけど，言えなかった表現」を，「こう言えばいいのかな」と，ペアで相談してみてください。この表現でいいかな…と迷うことがあったら，先生に言ってください。また，どうしてもわからない場合も遠慮なく，先生に言ってください。時間は3分間とります。

Ss：（ペアで共有し合う）

S1：先生。「朝ごはん食べる時間がない」って何て言うんですか。

T：今日だけ？

S1：いつも。

T：Oh, my god! You need to eat breakfast every morning. 「時間がない」は？

S1：No time.

T：そうだね。I have （ゆっくり言ってあげる）no time

S1：I have no time

T：「食べる時間」だから，to eat.

S1：to eat.

T：I have no time to eat. となります。毎朝なら，every morning を付けるといいかな。

S1：I have no time to eat every morning.

T：そう。他には？

S2：「漬物」

T：日本語でも，「ピクルス」って言うよね。英語で，pickle と言います。

中間評価の方法③ 「コミュニケーションを図ろうとする状況」を指導・評価する。

「主体的に学習に取り組む態度」の向上を目指し，ある一定の期間，継続的に指導します。「相づちを打ちながら相手の話を聞く」ことや「相手の理解を確かめながら話をする」のように，コミュニケーションを円滑に行う方法の指導計画を作成し，活動後に，「相づちを打ちながらできた人？」と尋ね，手を挙げさせ，「では，次は，できるだけ，相づちを打ちながら Small Talk をしましょう」と目標を示してから，2回目の Small Talk に入るのもよいでしょう。

参考 『中学英語 実例でわかる！「主体的に学習に取り組む態度」の学習評価』（瀧沢広人 著 学陽書房）

中間評価の方法④ Small Talk シートに記録させる。

　次のような「Small Talk シート」を配付し，中間評価の時間に「言いたかったけど，言えなかった表現」を書かせたり，それを解決させたりします。「今日の目標」は，一斉に与える場合もありますが，個人の目標を書かせてもよいです。

Small Talk シート　今週のテーマ〔breakfast〕
　　Name _____　　Date：_____

【第1回】

今日の目標		
【言いたかったけど，言えなかった表現】		（調べてみたら？）
自己評価	①今日の目標は達成できましたか。	5　4　3　2　1
	②1分間，会話を続けられましたか。	5　4　3　2　1

４　生徒同士の Small Talk（2回目）（1分）

　生徒は，中間評価で得られた知識を用いたり，コミュニケーションの取り方についての目標を意識したりしながら，2回目の Small Talk に入ります。ペアを替え，前後でペアになります。

> T：O.K. Change your partners. Move your desks, 前後.
> Ss：（生徒は前後で机をくっつける）
> T：I'll give you one minute. Let's start.

:::留意点:::
　　2回目の Small Talk が終わったら，自己評価させます。「1回目と比べて，よりよく話せるようになりましたか」と投げかけるなど，向上的変容を確認します。

② Small Talk をこんな風に取り組んでみたら？

①テーマを毎回変えるのではなく，複数回続けてみたら？

　通常の Small Talk では，毎回テーマを変えます。しかし，テーマを毎回変えることなく，一定時期，同じテーマで話させたらどうでしょうか。必然的に，同じテーマで Small Talk を繰り返すので，その話題についての対話力が確実に身に付くかと思います。

　また，生徒も１日目にやったテーマで，２日目，３日目，４日目と続けていくので，安心感にもつながります。「今日もあのテーマだ」と思えば，「今日はどんなことを話そうかな」と，事前に話す内容を考えてくる生徒もいるかも知れません。

　英語教育で言ういわゆるリハーサル（rehearsal）です。話そうとすることを，頭の中や声に出して繰り返し言うことによって，言いたいことを短期的に記憶したり（維持リハーサル），頭の中にある既有知識同士を関連付けることにより，手続き記憶として長期記憶に保存したり（精緻化リハーサル）することになります。さらに，教師側も毎回テーマを考えずに済みます。

②目標を１分，２分，３分としてみたら？

　時間的な目標も大事です。Small Talk の継続時間を，先述の通り（p.10），中学１年生で１分，２年生で２分，３年生で３分と，教師も迷わず提示できる目安で，わかりやすくします。

　もちろん，中学１年生の３学期末で１分ですので，１学期は30秒，２学期は45秒のように設定し，「30秒できる」「45秒できる」「１分できた！」と思わせながらするとよいでしょう。

③ペアでなく，Small Talk を４人組でやってみたら？

　Small Talk の基本は，ペアで行います。しかし，時には４人組で行わせたらどうでしょうか。グループの中で，リーダーシップを取り，会話を組み立てていく生徒がいたり，話を聞いて，話題を広げる生徒がいたり，または，みんなが同じように話ができるように，発言を譲ったり，話題をふったりする生徒の姿が見られるでしょう。これも大切な会話力と考えます。もちろん，４人１組での Small Talk テストをすることも考えられます。

④「やり取り」でなく，Small Talk を「発表」にしてみたら？

　Small Talk は，どちらかと言うとペアによる「やり取り」をイメージします。しかし，そこを「発表」にすることもできます。Please tell me about your breakfast. と言えば，生徒は，朝食について語らなくてはいけません。いわゆる「発表」になります。

　机を向かい合わせ，ペアにします。窓側の生徒を立たせます。１分間，自分の朝食に関連する話をします。１分経ったら，教師がベルを鳴らし，今度は，廊下側の生徒が立って話をし

ます。それぞれが終わった後，30秒程，質疑応答させてもよいでしょう。

　この「発表」の活動を通じ，「内容を整理して話すこと」のできる生徒に育てます。

　急に，話すように言われ，瞬時に，話す内容を整理できる力を，育てていきたいです。もちろん，Small Talk だけで育てるのではなく，全授業を通じて，「伝えたいことを整理し」「どこから話すか，話す順序を考え」「必要に応じて，接続詞を用いる」等，「発表」のための練習は必要だと考えます。

　ペアで「発表」ができれば，4人1組で行うこともできます。話す順番を決め，1人ずつ立って話をします。1分経ったら，教師がベルを鳴らし，左隣の生徒が立って話をします。それぞれ終わった後に，質問タイムを設けてもよいでしょう。

⑤相手の発言をメモし，それを他者に伝えてみたら？

　通常，Small Talk は，口頭でのやり取りです。口頭ですので，終わったら残りません。

　そこで，記録に残す意味でも，Small Talk シート（p.13）を工夫し，そこに〔メモ欄〕を作ります。そして，相手の話したことを，メモしていきます。もちろんメモですので，単語や簡単な文で書き，関連のあることは，線で結ぶなど，マッピングをしていきます。

　すると，今度は，そのメモを見ながら，前後のペアに，伝えるという活動（reporting）が可能になります。また，メモを取ることで，相手の話をよく聞き，話の流れを理解したり，もう少し質問したいことも生まれてきたりするでしょう。何より，相手の話を聞いて，概要や要点を掴むよい練習になります。

⑥時間でペアを替え，多くの人と Small Talk をしてみたら？

　Small Talk の基本形は，生徒同士の Small Talk を，隣のペアで1回，前後のペアで1回，合計2回行うこととなっています。しかしある面，活動を多く繰り返すことで，技能が身に付くということもあります。そこで，例えば1分間の Small Talk の後，席を1つ移動し，異なる生徒と2回目，3回目，4回目と，連続的に行うパターンもあります。

　生徒の活動が多くなればなるほど，教師も生徒を観察する時間が長くなり，生徒の現状や課題が見つかり，その後の指導の手立てが見えてくるかと思います。

⑦時には，準備のある Small Talk や，タブレットを用いた Small Talk をしてみたら？

　Small Talk と言うと即興的な対話をイメージしますが，教師がテーマを提供した後，少し話す内容を整理する時間をとらせたらどうでしょうか。自分が話そうとすることをマッピングさせたり，箇条書きで書かせたりしてから，Small Talk に臨ませます。

　また，何か具体物や写真があると，人は話しやすかったり，話の内容をイメージしやすくなったりします。タブレットを用い，写真等を見せながらの Small Talk もよいでしょう。

③ Small Talk の評価

① Small Talk テストを行う。

「活動と評価」をセットにし，活動したら，何らかの方法で評価するとよいです。また，評価があることで，活動への取組が"真剣になる"という面があります。これは「テスト効果」と言われるもので，評価が無いと，徐々に活動がいい加減になったり，ふざけ始めたり，ただ無駄な時間が過ぎたりするということにもなっていきます。

そこで，Small Talk テストを行うことを宣言し，評価活動を行います。その際，評価基準をしっかり決めておきます。基本的には，「言語面」「内容面」「態度面」から評価を考えるとよいでしょう。もちろん，3つの観点全てを同時に評価する必要はありません。

（例1）【中学1年生　3学期】

目標		過去の出来事について，伝え合うことができる。		
評価規準		過去の出来事について，伝え合っている。		
		【言語面】 （知識・技能）	【内容面】 （思考・判断・表現）	【態度面】 （主体的に学習に取り組む態度）
評価基準	a	過去形を<u>正確に</u>用いて表現する技能が身に付いている。	過去の出来事について，<u>知りたいことを尋ねたり，必要な情報を伝え合ったり</u>している。	過去の出来事について，<u>質問したり，詳しく話そうとしたり</u>している。
	b	過去形を<u>概ね</u>正確に用いて表現する技能が身に付いている。	過去の出来事について，<u>概ね</u>伝え合うことができている。	過去の出来事について，<u>概ね</u>伝え合おうとしている。
	c	過去形を正しく用いる技能が身に付いていない。	過去の出来事と伝え合うための情報量が少ない。	発言量が少なく，過去の出来事を伝えようという気持ちが見られない。

毎回の Small Talk で，生徒に自己評価させていってもよいでしょう。

＜自己評価＞ （例）

項目	6/1	/	/	/
①過去形を正確に用いて質問したり，答えたりすることができましたか。	b			
②相手のことをよく知るために，過去の出来事について，詳しく質問したり，答えたりしましたか。	b			
③相手のことをよく知るために，過去の出来事について，詳しく質問したり，答えたりしようとしましたか。	b			

②評価規準・評価基準を事前に示す。

　評価をする際，よく議論になるのが，評価規準・評価基準を，事前に示した方がいいか，直前に示した方がいいか，それとも途中で示した方がいいかという提示のタイミングです。私の結論は，「事前に示す」です。あらかじめ事前に示し，それで評価することを伝えます。

　事前に示すということは，教師側に，こうなって欲しいという理想がなくてはいけません。それが目標となり，その理想を持って，指導に当たります。

　しかしながら，理想を持つためには，生徒の実態を知らなくてはいけません。生徒の実態を知るために，試しに Small Talk をさせ，もし，「対話が1分間，続かないなあ」と思えば，目標を「テーマに即し，対話を1分間以上継続できる」とし，評価規準・評価基準を設定していきます。

　先ほどは，3つの観点全てを取り上げましたが，指導の重点を掲げ，例えば，「態度面」だけに重点を絞り，評価規準・評価基準を作成することもできます。

（例2）【中学1年生　2学期】　評価の観点（主体的に学習に取り組む態度）

目標		相手意識を持ち，対話を1分間以上継続することができる。
評価規準		相手意識を持ち，対話を1分間以上継続しようとしている。
評価基準	a	間が空かないよう，相づちを打ったり，相手に質問したり，話題を深めたりしようとしている。
	b	間が空かないよう，相づちを打ちながら，対話を継続しようとしている。
	c	相づちが打てず，対話が途切れる。

　今回は，「相づちを打つことができること」をb基準としていますが，相づちが自然と出るようになったら，次は，「話題を深めながら，対話を1分間継続している」を評価規準とし，それをb基準としていくとよいでしょう。そして，a基準を例えば，「話題を深めるために，相手に質問するとともに，質問に答えたら1文付け加えるなど，詳しく話している」と，次の段階を示します。

（例3）【中学1年生　3学期】　評価の観点（主体的に学習に取り組む態度）

目標		相手のことを詳しく知るために，話題を深めながら，対話を1分間継続することができる。
評価規準		相手のことを詳しく知るために，話題を深めながら，対話を1分間継続しようとしている。
評価基準	a	相手に質問するとともに，質問に答えたら1文付け加えるなど，詳しく話そうとしている。
	b	相手に様々な質問を投げかけ，対話を継続しようとしている。
	c	話題を深める質問ができていない。

　これらを集中的に Small Talk での目標とし，継続的に指導・評価していきます。

2 Small Talk に役立つ！「すらすら英会話」のやり方

① Small Talk 版「すらすら英会話」の活用法

Small Talk の力を付けていくために，Small Talk で「すらすら英会話」を用います。
目的は，以下の2つです。

---
①テーマに即した基本的な質問にすらすら答えたり，尋ねたりする力を育てる。
②会話を継続させたり，発展させたりする方法を学ぶ。

単発な Small Talk でなく，意図的・継続的な10分間の Small Talk として，指導計画に位置付けます。

② Small Talk 版「すらすら英会話」の進め方

ワークシート（次ページ）を配り，次の手順で行います。

指導手順

❶教師の後に繰り返させる。（1分）

基本は，ワークシート通りに，すらすら言えることをまずは目指します。会話調になっていますので，やっているうちに，だんだんと覚えてしまうかと思います。

T : Look at the handout. Repeat after me.
　　What did you eat for breakfast?
Ss: What did you eat for breakfast?
T : I ate rice, *miso* soup and egg.
Ss: I ate rice, *miso* soup and egg.
　⋮

18

中学1年 すらすら英会話
su ra su ra ei kai wa

What did you eat for breakfast?

Today's Point 話題をつなげて会話を継続させましょう。

① What did you eat for breakfast?

❶ I ate rice, *miso* soup and egg.

② Wow, nice. What *miso* soup did you eat?

❷ I ate *tofu* and seaweed. *Tofu* and seaweed *miso* soup is my favorite.

③ How do you like your eggs?

❸ I like my eggs sunny-side up.

④ Good, I like it too. What else do you eat?

❹ I eat *natto*.

⑤ Oh, do you like *natto*?

❺ Yes, I love it. It's very healthy.

⑥ Do you eat bread for breakfast?

❻ No. I do not eat bread for breakfast. I always eat rice.

⑦ What time do you usually have breakfast?

❼ I have breakfast around 7:00.

⑧ Do you have breakfast every day?

❽ Of course, I do. Having breakfast is very important.

⑨ I think so too. What time do you usually eat breakfast?

❾ I usually eat breakfast around 7:00.

⑩ Do you brush your teeth after breakfast?

❿ Of course, I do.

Useful Expressions

☐ Wow, nice. (わあ，いいね)

☐ How do you like your eggs? (卵はどう食べる？)

☐ I liked it too. (私もそれが好きです)

19

❷教師が左側，生徒が右側を読んでいく。（1分）

次に，教師と生徒で役割音読をします。単純に，教師が左側，生徒が右側を読むように指示します。

T: 先生が左側，みんなは右側を読んでいきます。

　　What did you eat for breakfast?

Ss: I ate rice, *miso* soup and egg.

T: Wow, nice. What *miso* soup did you eat?

Ss: I ate *tofu* and seaweed. *Tofu* and seaweed *miso* soup is my favorite.

T: How do you like your eggs?

Ss: I like my eggs sunny-side up.

T: Good. I like it too. What else do you eat?

Ss: I eat *natto*.

　　⋮

この状態で，すらすら言えない生徒も，練習を繰り返していくことで，だんだんと言えるようになってきます。

終わったら，今と逆のことをします。

T: 先生が右側，みんなは左側を読んでいきます。Ready go!

Ss: What did you eat for breakfast?

T: I ate rice, *miso* soup and egg.

Ss: Wow, nice. What *miso* soup did you eat?

T: I ate *tofu* and seaweed. *Tofu* and seaweed *miso* soup is my favorite.

　　⋮

---

❸ペアで読み合う。（1分）

教師と生徒でやったことを，生徒同士でやらせます。ジャンケンをして，勝った人が左側，負けた人が右側を読むように指示します。

T: O.K. Next, do *janken*.

Ss: （ジャンケンをする）

T: Winners?（ジャンケンに勝った生徒は手を挙げる）Read the left part.

　　Losers?（ジャンケンに負けた生徒は手を挙げる）Read the right part.

> Ready start.
> Ss:（読み合う）

　この時，とかく，自分のことで言わせたくなってしまいますが，まずは，ワークシートに書かれたものを，そのまま読み合うようにします。

❹ペアを替えて読み合う。（3分）

　ある程度の時間で，だいたい40秒くらいしたら，ペアを替えます。廊下側の生徒は1つ左に席を移動します。すると，新しいペアと出会います。出会ったら，ジャンケンをして，勝った人が左側，負けた人が右側を読んでいきます。

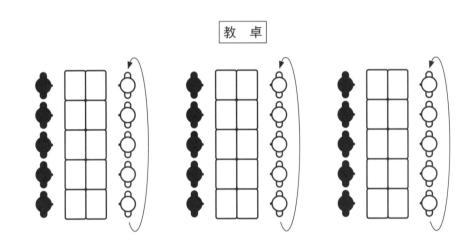

> T: Students on the right, move one seat back.
> Ss:（教卓に向かって右側＝廊下側の生徒は1つ席を移動する）

　席移動も最初は戸惑うかと思いますが，慣れるとスムーズに移動できるようになります。語彙や表現に慣れさせた状態で，Small Talk にはいります。

　Small Talk 版「すらすら英会話」は，Small Talk で使える表現を提示するほか，Small Talk の展開の仕方も同時に理解させることができます。こんな風に話を持っていくことができるという見本となります。

　また，各 Small Talk で目標を持って取り組めるように，point を設け，「 Today's Point 話題をつなげて会話を継続させましょう。」のように，目標設定を入れています。

column
コラム

....
Small Talk のパフォーマンス評価
....

　評価はとても大事です。指導する前に，どのようなことで評価するのか考えておきます。そして，生徒と事前に共有しておきます。テストをしてから，「こんな視点で評価しました」ではなく，事前に伝えるべきです。そのためには，教師側で，しっかりした評価規準及び，評価基準を持っていなくてはいけません。

　Small Talk では，「今日は，『答えたら１文付け足して詳しく話す』ようにしましょう」と，目標を１つ示し，場合によっては，単元内は同じ目標で継続していくと，その技能が高まります。そして単元末に，その技能ができているかどうか，身に付いているかどうかを確認・評価していくのもよいでしょう。

　もちろん，身に付いている状態にするためには，単元末だけでなく，3か月後，6か月後，9か月後まで，その技能が継続してできているか見届ける必要があります。

【話すこと（やり取り）の評価項目】

区分	評価項目	評価の観点
言語面	□語や語句，表現，文法を正確に用いている。 □発音はアクセント，イントネーションが正確である。	知識・技能
内容面	□語や語句，表現，文法を適切に用いている。 □繰り返したり，相づちを打ったりする等，会話を継続している。 □答えたら，1文付け足し，詳しく話している。 □質問されたら同じ質問を相手にもしている。 □相手をよく知るために質問したり，確認したりしている。 □質問するだけでなく，自分のことも伝えている。 □話題を深めたり，広げたりしている。 □相手がうまく表現できない時に，語や語句を補い，理解を示している。 □内容を整理して話している。	思考・判断・表現
態度面	□身体を相手の方に向け，相手の目を見て話そうとしている。 □ジェスチャーを用い，伝えようとしている。 □相手に聞こえる声量で話そうとしている。 □うまく伝えられない時に，他の表現で伝えられないか考えて話そうとしている。	主体的に学習に取り組む態度

Chapter 2

中学1年で扱いたい！
トピック別
「すらすら英会話」
15

1 【接続期①】自己紹介
Get to know each other

「お互いを知る」を目的に，自己紹介を行います。自己紹介は，様々な表現を使わせることができ，生徒の発話力が確認できます。小学校での英語を振り返らせましょう。

文法事項	現在形 (be 動詞・一般動詞)　疑問詞 (What, How, When, Where)

主な表現　I am ＿＿＿. My name is ＿＿＿. Please call me 〜. I'm from ＿＿＿.
How do you spell your name? What's your favorite 〜?
My favorite 〜 is ＿＿＿. I like ＿＿＿. I play ＿＿＿.
When is your birthday? My birthday is ＿＿＿. Where do you live?　等

実施時期　中学1年　4月中旬〜5月中旬

留意点　小学校で英語を学んだ生徒は，中学校に入ってまず始めに不安を感じるのは，「英語が読めないこと」だと言われます。そこで最初は「接続期①〜⑤」(pp.24-33) を口頭でやり取りをするとよいでしょう。その後，英文を読むことにだんだん慣れてきた段階で「これらの質問にはすらすらと答えられるといいね」と言ってワークシートを渡し，時期を見て練習をさせます。

応用・発展　Common Things
　　　☞ Find common things with your partner.〔共通点を見つけよう〕
Tell about Your Partner
　　　☞ How much do you know about your partner?〔相手のことを言い当てよう〕

Teacher's Talk

T : Hello, everyone. I'm Hiroto Takizawa. H-i-r-o-t-o, T-a-k-i-z-a-w-a. My name is Hiroto Takizawa. Please call me Takizawa-*sensei*. I am from Tokyo. I am 58 years old. My birthday is January 19th. My favorite food is *natto*. I usually eat it for breakfast. I like growing vegetables. Look.（写真）I grow these vegetables. Growing vegetables makes me relaxed.

T : What is your name? (S1：My name is ....) Your name is .... Thank you.

T : When is your birthday? (S1：My birthday is ....) Your birthday is ....

T : What's your favorite food? (S2：My favorite food is *sushi*.) Oh, *sushi*? It's delicious.

T : O.K. How much do you know about your friend? Let's ask your partner.

中学1年 すらすら英会話
su ra su ra ei kai wa

Get to know each other.

Today's Point 相手のことをよく知るために，たくさん質問しましょう。

① Hello. How do you do?

① How do you do?

② My name is Yuki Minami. What is your name?

② My name is Hiroto Takizawa.

③ How do you spell your name?

③ H-i-r-o-t-o, T-a-k-i-z-a-w-a.

④ What can I call you?

④ Please call me Hiroto.

⑤ Where are you from?

⑤ I'm from Tokyo.

⑥ Where do you live?

⑥ I live in Gifu.

⑦ What is your favorite food?

⑦ My favorite food is *natto*.

⑧ What sport do you like?

⑧ I like volleyball.

⑨ When is your birthday?

⑨ My birthday is January 19th.

⑩ How old are you?

⑩ I'm 13 years old.

⑪ What subjects do you like?

⑪ I like English and science.

⑫ What do you want to be in the future?

⑫ I want to be a pilot in the future.

⑬ Nice talking with you.

⑬ Nice talking with you too.

Tips !

見なくても，すらすら言えるようになったかな？
右側を読めば，そのまま自己紹介文になるね。

25

2 【接続期②】果物や野菜
Fruit or Vegetable

　果物や野菜の話題は，比較的 Small Talk にしやすいトピックと言えます。sweet（甘い）や，sour（酸っぱい），salty（しょっぱい），juicy（みずみずしい），soft/light and warm（ほくほくしている）等の味の言い方も同時に教える機会となります。

文法事項	一般動詞（現在形）　疑問詞（What, Why, Where）
主な表現	What fruits do you like?　I like ＿＿＿.　Why do you like ＿＿＿?
	Do you like ～?　What vegetables do you like?
	Where do you go to pick apples?
	What vegetable do you like the best?
	What kind of salad do you like?　等
実施時期	中学1年　4月中旬～5月中旬
留意点	「私は～が好きです」と言う時は，たいてい名詞は複数形にしますが，丸ごと1個食べないような大きいもの（例：スイカなど）は，I like watermelon. と単数で言います。その場合，代名詞も It is juicy. のように it で受けます。
応用・発展	Favorite Dessert

　　　 ☞ What is your favorite dessert?〔好きなスイーツは何？〕
　　　Favorite Drink
　　　 ☞ What kind of drinks do you like?〔何の飲み物が好き？〕

Teacher's Talk

T : Good morning. This is my dinner last night. I ate spaghetti. Look.（写真）
　 I always eat salad. It is healthy. I like almost all kinds of vegetables. I like cucumbers, mushrooms, carrots, lettuce, cabbage, cherry tomatoes, tomatoes.（写真）But I do not like celery.（写真）I do not like the taste.
　 What vegetables do you like?

S1: I like potatoes ....

T : What fruits do you like? I like bananas. They are not expensive, but my favorite fruit is watermelon. It is juicy and sweet. I eat it only in summer. What fruits do you like?

Ss: I like ....

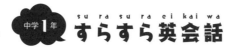

Let's talk about 'Fruit' or 'Vegetable.'

Today's Point Small Talk は「あいさつ」で始め,終わりは気の利いた一言を言いましょう。

① What fruits do you like?
❶ I like watermelon and grapes.

② Why do you like watermelon?
❷ It's juicy and sweet.
　I like juicy fruits.
　I like peaches too.
　But they are expensive.

③ Do you like apples?
❸ Yes, I do. I go to pick apples every fall.

④ Where do you go to pick apples?
❹ I always go to Gunma.

⑤ Do you like lemons?
❺ No. I don't like lemons.

⑥ Why not?
❻ They are too sour.

⑦ What vegetables do you like?
❼ I like all kinds.

⑧ What vegetable do you like the best?
❽ I like cucumbers the best.

⑨ Why?
❾ Because they are juicy and crumchy.

⑩ What kind of salad do you like?
❿ I like potato salad.

⑪ Nice talking with you.
⓫ I enjoyed talking with you too.

Useful Expressions 終わりの言葉を工夫して言いましょう。

☐ Nice talking with you.（あなたとお話できて素敵な時間でした）
☐ I enjoyed talking with you.（あなたとお話できて楽しかったです）
☐ Have a good day!（よい1日でありますように！）

3 【接続期③】あなたの１日
My Daily Life

「日課」の表現も，生徒は小学校で学習してきます。しかし，慣れ親しむまでには到達していないかと思いますので，既習事項を想起させながら Small Talk を行いましょう。

文法事項	現在形（一般動詞）　疑問詞（What, When）
主な表現	What time do you usually get up? What do you do after breakfast? Do you walk to school?　When do you take a bath?　等
実施時期	中学１年　４月中旬～５月中旬
留意点	黒板にイラストを貼り，語句を確認してから行うとよいでしょう。 ① get up　② have/eat breakfast　③ brush my teeth　④ change clothes ⑤ go to school　⑥ go home　⑦ get home　⑧ have/eat dinner　⑨ take a bath　⑩ watch TV/YouTube　⑪ read books　⑫ listen to music　⑬ study ⑭ do my homework　⑮ play video games/the piano　⑯ go to bed
応用・発展	Weekend ☞ How do you spend your weekends?〔週末はどう過ごすの？〕 Morning Routine ☞ What is your morning routine?〔朝の日課はどんな感じ？〕

Teacher's Talk

T: Look at this.（「6:00」という時刻を見せる）This is my wake-up time. I always get up at 6:00 or before 6:00. After I wake up, I take a bath. I like taking a bath, so I take a bath twice a day, in the morning and in the evening. Then, I have breakfast. I go to school at 6:30. I come to school at 7:00. I have tennis morning practice, then I start teaching. What time do you usually get up?

S1: I usually get up at 6:00.

T: Oh, you too? That's very early. What do you do after you wake up?

S1: I change my clothes and have breakfast.

T: What time do you go to school?

S1: I go to school at 7:30.（他，数名の生徒と対話する）

T: Thank you. After school, I get home around 7:00. I take a bath and have dinner. I watch TV, read books, and do some work, then I usually go to bed at 11:00. What time do you usually go to bed?

Let's talk about 'My Daily Life.'

Today's Point 相手が言ったことを繰り返してみましょう。

① What time do you usually get up?
❶ I usually get up at 6:30.

② <u>6:30?</u> What time do you eat breakfast?
❷ I eat breakfast at 6:50.

③ What do you eat for breakfast?
❸ I always eat rice and *miso* soup.

④ What do you do after breakfast?
❹ I brush my teeth and change clothes.

⑤ What time do you go to school?
❺ I go to school at 7:30.

⑥ Do you walk to school?
❻ <u>Walk to school?</u> No. I go to school by bike.

⑦ What time do you get home?
❼ I get home at 4:30.

⑧ <u>At 4:30?</u> What do you do after that?
❽ I play video games with my friends. I listen to music. I watch YouTube. I go to *juku* on Wednesday and Friday.

⑨ <u>You go to *juku*?</u> What do you study?
❾ I study math and English.

⑩ When do you take a bath?
❿ <u>When?</u> I take a bath before dinner.

⑪ What time do you go to bed?
⓫ I go to bed at 10:30.

Useful Expressions

〔対話を続ける方法〕 ①繰り返す ②相づちを打つ ③感想を言う ④質問する

☐ I usually get up at 6:30. ― 6:30?（単語で繰り返す）
☐ Do you walk to school? ― Walk to school?（語句で繰り返す）
☐ I go to *juku* on Wednesday and Friday. ― You go to *juku*?（文で繰り返す）

4 【接続期④】 小学校の思い出
School Memories

　生徒は小学校で，My best memory を学習してきます。校区によっては，複数の小学校が1つの中学校に集まることがあります。どんな小学校生活を送ってきたのでしょうか。

文法事項　現在形 (be 動詞・一般動詞)　過去形 (be 動詞・一般動詞)
　　　　　　疑問詞 (What, Where, What else, How, How many)

主な表現　What is your best memory?　Where did you go?　What did you enjoy?
　　　　　　What else did you enjoy?　What did you do?　What did you eat?
　　　　　　How was it?　Did you go to ～?　How many days did you stay?
　　　　　　What is your second-best memory?　等

実施時期　中学1年　4月中旬～5月中旬

留意点　What school events did you have in your elementary school? と尋ね，どんな学校行事があったのか確認してから，Teacher's Talk に入るといいです。

応用・発展　Good Memories in My Life
　　　　　☞What are your good memories in your life?〔よい思い出は何？〕
　　　　　Best Memory in My Life
　　　　　☞What is the best memory in your life?〔一番の思い出は何？〕

Teacher's Talk

T: Last year, you were elementary school students. What is your best memory? My best memory is the school trip. We went to Nikko by bus. We stayed for two nights. We went to Toshogu, and I saw three monkeys. Don't look. Don't talk. Don't listen. (写真) I also saw a sleeping cat. (写真) It was very small. Then I clapped my hands, and I heard the dragon's voice. I saw a big waterfall too. It is Kegon Fall. (写真) I had a good time.

T: What's your best memory?　　　S1: My best memory is the Sports Day.

T: What did you enjoy?　　　　　S1: I enjoyed the class relay.

T: Wow, did you win the relay?　　S1: Yes, our red team won first place.

T: Wow, congratulations!
　 How about you?　　　　　　　S2: My best memory is swimming meet.

T: Are you good at swimming?　　S2: Yes. I got second place.

Let's talk about 'School Memories.'

Today's Point 積極的に相づちを打ってみましょう。

① What is your best memory?

❶ My best memory is the school trip.

② <u>Oh, me too.</u> Where did you go?

❷ We went to Kamakura and Hakone.

③ What did you enjoy?

❸ I enjoyed riding on a boat.

④ <u>I see.</u> What else did you enjoy?

❹ I enjoyed free time at Komachi Street.

⑤ What did you do?

❺ I enjoyed shopping and eating sweets.

⑥ What did you eat?

❻ I ate a crepe.

⑦ You ate a crepe? How was it?

❼ It was great!

⑧ Did you go to Kamakura Daibutsu?

❽ Yes, I did. It was big.

⑨ <u>Well,</u> how many days did you stay?

❾ We stayed for one night.

⑩ Only one night? What did you enjoy?

❿ I enjoyed playing cards.
　 I enjoyed talking with my friends.

⑪ <u>Right!</u>
　 What is your second-best memory?

⓫ My second-best memory is the Sports Day. Our team won the relay.

Useful Expressions

〔対話を続ける方法〕　①繰り返す　②相づちを打つ　③感想を言う　④質問する

☐ I see.（わかりました）　　☐ Me too.（私も）　　☐ You too?↗（あなたも？）

☐ Really?（本当？）　　　　☐ Uh-huh.（うんうん）　☐ Is that right?↘（そうなんだ？）

☐ Right.（そうなんだよ）　　☐ Tell me more.（もう少し話して）　☐ Well …,（えーと）

5 【接続期⑤】 将来の夢
Dreams for the Future

　生徒の多くは，What do you want to be? ― I want to be a/an 〜. のやり取りは慣れ親しんできていると思われます。want to を使って，やりたいことを引き出しましょう。

文法事項	現在形（一般動詞）　疑問詞（What, Why, Where, How about）
主な表現	What do you want to be in the future?　Why do you want to be a pilot? Where do you want to go?　Why do you want to go to France? How about Italy?　What do you want to do? Do you want to eat pizza?　Can you play the piano? I hope your dreams come true.　等
実施時期	中学1年　4月中旬〜5月中旬
留意点	夢を語る時は，将来なりたい職業だけでなく，将来やりたいことも話題にできます。例えば，I want to have a dog.（犬を飼いたい）や，I want to win the soccer game.（サッカーの試合で勝ちたい）など，夢はいくらでも語ることができます。
応用・発展	This Weekend 　☞ What do you want to do this weekend?〔今週末やりたいこと〕 Dreams 　☞ What dreams do you have this year?〔今年はどんな夢がある？〕

Teacher's Talk

T: Hello, this is a picture when I was a child. Where am I? （写真）（Ss：どの子が先生であるか指さす）This is me. When I was small, I wanted to be a baker. I wanted to bake bread. When I was an elementary school student, I liked trains. I wanted to be a train conductor. Look. Where am I? （写真）When I was a junior high school student, I wanted to be a teacher. What subject did I like?

Ss: English? Science? Math? Music?

T: I liked math very much, so I wanted to be a math teacher. When I was in the third grade at junior high school, I had a chance to talk with a foreign lady in English. Then I became to like English. I began to think that I wanted to be an English teacher. And now I am here. What do you want to be in the future?

中学**1**年 **すらすら英会話** (su ra su ra ei kai wa)

Let's talk about 'Dreams for the Future.'

Today's Point アイコンタクトをとりながら，しっかり相づちも打ちましょう。

① Do you have dreams for the future? ❶ Yes, I do.

② What do you want to be in the future? ❷ I want to a pilot or a teacher.

③ Great! Why do you want to be a pilot? ❸ I want to visit many places.

④ Wow, nice. Where do you want to go? ❹ I want to go to France and Italy.

⑤ Why do you want to go to France? ❺ I want to see the Eiffel Tower and the Mont Saint-Michel.

⑥ I see. How about Italy? What do you want to do? ❻ Well ..., I want to see the Leaning Tower of Pisa.

⑦ Do you want to eat pizza? ❼ Of course. I want to eat pizza.

⑧ Why do you want to be a teacher? ❽ Because I like children.

⑨ Do you want to be an elementary school teacher? ❾ I want to be a kindergarten teacher. I like small children.

⑩ Oh, good! Can you play the piano? ❿ Yes, a little. I practice the piano every day.

⑪ Cool. I hope your dreams come true. ⓫ Thank you. I hope so too.

Useful Expressions 相づち表現を積極的に使ってみましょう。

☐ Great. （いいね） ☐ Nice. （素敵ね／いいね） ☐ I see. （わかりました）

☐ Well ..., （えーと） ☐ Of course. （もちろん） ☐ Good! （いいね！）

☐ Cool. （いいね／かっこいいね／おしゃれ） ☐ I hope so too. （私もそう期待します）

33

6 部活動は何部？　趣味は？
Club Activity or Hobbies

　生徒は小学校の英語授業で，I want to join the soccer club. や，I want to enjoy the Sports Day. などで，中学校でやりたいことや，希望を語る言語活動を行ってきます。部活動に所属しない生徒は，放課後の過ごし方や，何をするのが好きなのか話題にします。

文法事項	現在形（be 動詞・一般動詞）疑問詞（What, How, When, How many）
主な表現	Do you belong to the club activity?　What club do you belong to? How do you like your team?　When do you practice rughy? How many days do you practice it in a week? What do you like to do in your free time?　等
実施時期	中学1年　5月下旬
留意点	教科担任の英語教師は，教えている生徒が何部に入っているのか知らないことがあります。だからこそ，尋ねる目的が生まれます。教師の知りたいことを素直に尋ねるところに言語活動が生まれます。
応用・発展	After School 　　☞ What do you do after school?〔放課後はどう過ごしているの？〕 Free Time 　　☞ What do you like to do in your free time?〔暇な時，何する？〕

Teacher's Talk

T : Good morning. Do you belong to an after school club? What club do you belong to? When I was a junior high school student, I belonged to the soccer team. I practiced soccer very hard, and I enjoyed playing soccer. I made good friends there. At high school, I played soccer too, and at university, 大学で, at university, I played karate. I liked martial arts, 格闘技, martial arts.
　　What club do you belong to?

S1: Tennis.

T : Oh, tennis? How is the tennis team? ... Do you like it?

S1: Yes.

T : When do you play tennis?

S1: I play tennis on Monday, Tuesday, Wednesday, and Friday.

中学1年 すらすら英会話

Let's talk about 'Club Activity' or 'Hobbies.'

Today's Point 答えたら，できるだけ詳しく話すようにしましょう。

① Do you belong to the club activity?

❶ Yes. I belong to the rugby team.

② How do you like your team?

❷ I like my team very much.
My teammates are kind.
My team is strong.
We practice it very hard.

③ How many members do you have on your team?

❸ We have 13 7th graders on our team.
We have 8 8th graders.
We have 10 9th graders.
We have 31 players on our team in total.

④ Awesome! How many days do you practice rugby in a week?

❹ Five days a week. We practice it from Monday to Friday.

⑤ So many? What are you good at?

❺ I'm good at running.

⑥ How fast can you run?

❻ I can run 100m for 13.5 seconds.

⑦ Amazing! Are you serious?

❼ Yes. I'm serious.

⑧ No way! By the way, what do you like to do in your free time?

❽ I like playing video games.

⑨ What else do you like to do?

❾ I like drawing pictures.

Useful Expressions 相手の話に反応し，会話を継続させていきましょう。

☐ Amazing! / Awesome!（すごいね）　　　　☐ So many?（そんなにたくさん？）

☐ Are you serious? / Really?（本当に？／マジで？）　☐ I'm serious.（本気です／真面目です）

☐ No way!（信じられない！）　　　　　　　☐ By the way,（ところで）

35

7 ペットは何か飼っているの？
My Pet

ペットは家族の大切な一員です。特に，自分が飼っている動物に愛着を持ち，それを友だちに伝えたい生徒もいることでしょう。どんなペットを飼っているのか知る機会としましょう。

文法事項	現在形（一般動詞）　疑問詞（What, Where, How many, How old）
主な表現	Do you have any pets?　What pets do you have? How many dogs do you have?　Are they indoor dogs? What are the names of your dogs?　How old are Koro and Jiji? In human years, how old are they?　When do you walk them?　等
実施時期	中学1年　6月上旬
留意点	動物が好きでない生徒には，好きでない理由や，もし動物を飼うとしたらどんな動物がいいかなどを話題にしてもいいでしょう。

応用・発展	Zoo
	  ☞ What do you want to see at the zoo?〔動物園に行ったら何を見たい？〕
	Animals
	  ☞ What kinds of animals do you like?〔どんな動物が好き？〕

Teacher's Talk

T : Look! This is Mr.Otani. What pet does he have?（Ss: Dog!）Right. What is the name of his dog?（Ss: デコピン）Yes. Do you have pets? I used to have pets. Can you guess? I had fish, birds, chickens, a rabbit, a catfish, ナマズ, a catfish, and hamsters. But now, I do not keep any pets. I like to take a trip, so I cannot keep animals. Do you have any pets?

S1: Yes.

T : What pets do you have?

S1: I have a dog.

T : What is the name of your dog?

S1: Merry.

T : A cute name. Who named it?

S1: My mother named it.

Let's talk about 'Pets' or 'Animals.'

Today's Point 相手のことをよく知るために，たくさん質問しましょう。

① Do you have any pets?   ❶ Yes, I do.

② What pets do you have?   ❷ I have dogs.

③ Dogs? How many dogs do you have?   ❸ I have two dogs.

④ Are they indoor dogs?   ❹ Yes, they are house dogs.

⑤ What are the names of your dogs?   ❺ They are Koro and Jiji.

⑥ Nice names. Who named them?   ❻ I'm not sure, but maybe, my mother named them.

⑦ Is that so? How old are they?   ❼ Koro is 8 years old, and Jiji is 12.

⑧ In human years, how old are they?   ❽ Koro is 48 years old, and Jiji is 64.

⑨ Do you like animals?   ❾ Yes, I do. I like small animals.

⑩ I feel the same. What pets do you want to have?   ❿ Let's see, I want to have a hamster.

⑪ Cute! I used to have hamsters.   ⓫ Yes, they are lovely.

Useful Expressions 様々な言葉をはさみ，会話を継続させましょう。

☐ I'm not sure, but …. (よくわからないけど…)

☐ Maybe. (たぶん)

☐ Is that so? (そうなんだ)

☐ I feel the same. (そうですよね。私もそう思います)

☐ Let's see, … (えーと)

☐ Cute! (かわいいね！)

8 好きな食べ物は何？
Favorite Dish

　食べ物の話題は身近で好きな話題の１つです。食べ物の写真を見せるだけで，生徒は盛り上がるでしょう。中学生にもなれば，食べ物から色々な話題へ発展させることもできます。

| 文法事項 | 現在形（一般動詞）　疑問詞 (What, What kind of, Where, How often) |

| 主な表現 | I like ＿＿＿．　Do you like ＿＿＿？　What kind of ＿＿＿ do you like? |

What is your favorite dish?　What does it taste?

Where do you go to eat ＿＿＿？　How often do you eat ＿＿＿？

What do you want to eat tonight?　等

| 実施時期 | 中学１年　６月下旬 |

| 留意点 | 世界には，様々な食文化があり，それぞれ味や見た目に特徴があります。日本食は，海外の人たちから見ると，Colorful and beautiful. と言われ，食材の色のバランスや見た目の美しさを大事にします。各国にはそれぞれ独自の食文化がありますが，他国の食文化を尊重する生徒を育てていきたいです。 |

| 応用・発展 | Cooking |

　　　☞ What do you cook?〔どんな料理を作る？〕

Going Eat Out

　　　☞ Do you like to eat out?〔外食は好き？〕

Teacher's Talk

T : Good morning. Let's talk about 'food.' What is your favorite dish? I like all kinds of dish, but my favorite food is *natto*.（写真）I always eat it for breakfast. It is sticky, but it's healthy. I like egg for breakfast too.（写真）

I like curry and rice too. I like it because it's easy to eat. 食べやすい。It's easy to eat. There are many kinds of food in the world such as Western food, Italian food, Spanish food, Vietnamese food, Chinese food, Indonesian food, Korean food.（写真）They are delicious. What is your favorite dish?

S1: I like pasta.

T : You like pasta. I like napolitana. What kind of pasta do you like?

S1: I like vongole.

T : Why?

Let's talk about 'Favorite Dish.'

Today's Point 積極的に話題を見つけて対話しましょう。

① What is your favorite dish? ❶ I like curry and rice.

② I like it too. Why do you like it? ❷ It's delicious and easy to eat.

③ What kind of curry do you eat? ❸ I usually eat pork curry.

④ Do you like spicy curry? ❹ No, I like medium spicy.

⑤ What Japanese food do you like? ❺ I like all kinds of Japanese food.

⑥ What is your favorite food? ❻ My favorite food is *natto*. It's a healthy food.

⑦ What does it taste like? ❼ It smells bad, and it's sticky.

⑧ That is good. Do you eat *sushi*? ❽ Yes, but sometimes.

⑨ What *sushi* do you like? ❾ I like salmon and tuna.

⑩ Where do you usually eat *sushi*? ❿ I eat at Kaiten *sushi*.

⑪ Pardon? ⓫ A conveyor belt *sushi*.

⑫ What do you want to eat tonight? ⓬ I want to eat hamburger steak.

Useful Expressions 味覚の表現を覚えましょう。

☐ salty（しょっぱい）　　☐ sweet（甘い）　　☐ spicy/hot（辛い）　　☐ sour（酸っぱい）
☐ mild（口当たりのよい）　☐ bitter（苦い）　　☐ good/tasty/yummy（美味しい）
☐ greasy（脂っぽい）　　☐ crispy（パリパリ）　☐ light taste（あっさりした味）

9 夏休みは何したい？
Plans for My Summer Vacation

　Small Talk のテーマは，できるだけタイムリーなものにしたいです。夏休み前には，どんな風に夏を過ごしたいか尋ね合う Small Talk をしましょう。

文法事項	現在形（一般動詞）　不定詞（名詞的用法：want to）

主な表現	What do you want to do in your summer vacation?

　　　　　Do you go to the sea every summer?

　　　　　Who do you go with?

　　　　　Where do you want to go this year?

　　　　　What else do you want to do?　等

実施時期	中学1年　7月

留意点	夏休みのことを話題にする場合，どうしても未来表現を使いたくなりますが，生徒はまだ，未来表現は学習していません。そこで，「何したい？」（What do you want to do?）を用いることで，夏休みの過ごし方を伝え合うことができます。

応用・発展	This Weekend

　　　　　☞ What do you want to do this weekend?〔今週末の予定〕

　　　　　Today's Dinner

　　　　　☞ What do you want to eat for dinner tonight?〔今日の夕飯〕

Teacher's Talk

T : Today is July 10th. In two weeks, we'll have a long vacation. Do you have any plans for the summer vacation? I want to do four things.（ジェスチャー）First, I want to go to hot springs. I want to go to a hot spring in Aomori and enjoy staying there. Also, I want to enjoy barbeque. Second, I want to read many books. I have less time to read books these days, so I want to enjoy reading and relax. Third, I want to study English. I want to try English test this September, so I want to study it very hard. Lastly, I want to do exercise. I want to be healthy. What do you want to do this summer?

S1: Go to the sea.

T : Great! You want to go to the sea. Where do you want to go?

S1: I want to go to Niigata.

Let's talk about 'Plans for My Summer Vacation.'

Today's Point たくさん質問しましょう。

① Summer vacation is coming soon.

❶ Yes, it is.

② What do you want to do in your summer vacation?

❷ I want to go to the sea. I want to enjoy swimming.

③ Do you swim in the sea?

❸ Yes. I like snorkeling too.

④ Do you go to the sea every summer?

❹ Yes, I do.

⑤ Who do you go with?

❺ I go with my family and my cousins.

⑥ Where do you usually go?

❻ We usually go to Izu or Niigata.

⑦ Where do you want to go this year?

❼ I want to go to Okinawa this year.

⑧ Nice idea. What do you want to do there?

❽ I want to swim in the beautiful sea.

⑨ What else do you want to do?

❾ I want to practice and play soccer hard so I can be a very good player.

⑩ So, you want to practice soccer very hard.

❿ That's right. We have a soccer tournament every summer. We want to win the matches.

⑪ Good luck.

⓫ Thank you. I'll do my best.

Useful Expressions 励ます言葉を使ってみましょう。

☐ Good luck.（頑張って）　☐ You can do it.（君ならできる）　☐ Have fun.（楽しんで）
☐ Do your best.（ベストを尽くして）　☐ Don't give up.（あきらめずにね）
☐ Don't worry.（くよくよしないでね）　☐ I'm with you.（私がそばにいるから）

10 夏休みの思い出
Memories of Summer Vacation

　夏休みが終わったら，夏休みの思い出を語り合わせましょう。過去形を学習していなくても，生徒は小学校で，went, saw, ate, had, enjoyed, was などを用いて，言語活動を行ってきています。それらを思い出させながら行いましょう。

文法事項	現在形（be 動詞・一般動詞）　過去形（be 動詞・一般動詞） 不定詞（名詞的用法）
主な表現	How was your summer vacation? What did you do?　Who did you go with? How did you spend time at the camp?　What else did you do? How long did you stay there?　How was your tennis practice? What do you want to do next year?　等
実施時期	中学1年　9月
留意点	過去形は3学期に学習しますので，あくまでも表現として扱い，「『見る』はwatch，『見た』は watched と言うんだよ」程度の「語句」として，教えていきましょう。基本的な表現は，板書して，視覚情報を与えるとよいでしょう。
応用・発展	Last Summer 　☞ How did you spend last summer?〔昨年の夏はどう過ごした？〕 Long Weekend 　☞ What did you do over the long weekend?〔連休は何をした？〕

Teacher's Talk

T : Summer vacation is over. Did you enjoy your summer vacation? (Ss: Yes.)
　I enjoyed my summer vacation. My daughter's family came to my house and enjoyed barbeque in my garden.（写真）We ate beef and seafood. It was delicious. I went to a hot spring too. I had a good time at the hot spring.
　How did you spend your summer vacation?

S1: I had kendo practice. 合宿.

T : Oh, kendo camp. Where did you go?　S1: We went to Saitama.

T : How many days did you stay?　　　S1: We stayed three nights.

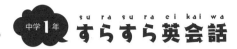

How did you spend your summer vacation?

Today's Point 相手の話に反応し，自分の思いや感想を言いましょう。

① Summer vacation is over.　　　　　❶ Yes. I'm sad.

② How was your summer vacation?　　❷ <u>Great!</u> I enjoyed it very much.

③ What did you do?　　　　　　　　❸ I went camping in Gifu.

④ <u>Interesting.</u> Who did you go with?　❹ I went with my family.

⑤ How did you spend time at the camp?　❺ I enjoyed cooking, eating and sleeping.

⑥ Did you swim in the river?　　　　❻ Yes. I enjoyed fishing too.

⑦ What else did you do?　　　　　　❼ Well, I went to my cousin's house.

⑧ Where is your cousin's house?　　　❽ In Gunma.

⑨ What did you do?　　　　　　　　❾ We enjoyed video games.

⑩ How long did you stay there?　　　❿ I stayed there for two nights.

⑪ How was your tennis practice?　　⓫ <u>Great!</u> We had a tennis match last week, and my team won the match.

⑫ <u>You did it!</u> What do you want to do next year?　⓬ I want to go to Hokkaido next year.

Useful Expressions

〔対話を続ける方法〕　①繰り返す　②相づちを打つ　③感想を言う　④質問する

☐ Great!（すごいね！）　　☐ Sounds good!（いい感じ！）　　☐ Well done.（よくやりました）
☐ Interesting.（興味深い／面白い）　☐ Fabulous.（素晴らしい）　☐ You did it!（やったね！）

11 友だちや先生について教えて！
Friends or Teachers

　3人称単数現在形の学習では，おそらく友だちや先生，有名人を題材に，タブレットを用いて紹介する活動をすると思います。その後，それをそのまま Small Talk でも行います。

| 文法事項 | 現在形 (be 動詞・一般動詞)　　3人称単数現在形 |

| 主な表現 | Tell me about your friends.　Does he have a pet? |

Does he play an instrument?　Does he have sisters or brothers?

Are they younger or older sister?　What do you like about him?

Where does he live?　What does he like?　What music does he like?

Does he sing songs?　等

| 実施時期 | 中学1年　10月 |

| 留意点 | よい機会ですので，人柄を表す語彙も教えるとよいでしょう。友だち紹介や先生紹介では，その人のよい面を見ることを教え，人のよいところを紹介することの大切さを伝え，指導しましょう。 |

| 応用・発展 | My Hero |

　　☞ Let me know about your hero.〔あこがれの人について教えて〕

Favorite Singer

　　☞ Who is your favorite singer?〔あなたの好きな歌手は誰?〕

Teacher's Talk

T : Look. This is Mr. Yamada. He is young and honest. He teaches social studies.
　　His class is very popular among students. He can play table tennis well.
　　He plays the drums too. He is a good musician.

T : Who is your homeroom teacher?　　　　S1: Ms. Suzuki.

T : What sport does she play?　　　　　　S2: She plays volleyball.

T : Where does she live?　　　　　　　　S3: She lives in Minami town.

T : What do you know about her?　　　　　S4: She has three children.

T : Wow, you know about her very much.
　　You are on the soccer team, right?　　　S5: Yes.
　　Who is the coach for the soccer team?　　S5: Mr. Tada.
　　Tell me about him.　　　　　　　　　S5: He teaches us soccer very hard.

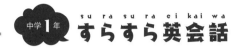

Let's talk about 'Friends' or 'Teachers.'

Today's Point 友だちのよいところを伝え合いましょう。

① Tell me about your friends.

❶ I have many friends.
 This is Taku in class 1-B.
 He can play basketball well.
 He is very cool.
 He runs fast.

② Does he have a pet?

❷ Yes, he does. He has a cat.

③ Does he play an instrument?

❸ Yes, he does. He plays the trumpet.

④ Does he have sisters or brothers?

❹ Yes, he does. He has two sisters.

⑤ Are they younger or older sisters?

❺ They are older sisters.

⑥ Where does he live?

❻ He lives near the shopping mall.

⑦ What does he like?

❼ He likes music.

⑧ What music does he like?

❽ He likes Vaundy.

⑨ Does he sing songs?

❾ Yes. He's good at singing.

⑩ What do you like about him?

❿ I like him because he helps me a lot.
 He's very kind.

Useful Expressions 人柄を表す表現を覚えましょう。

☐ kind（親切な／優しい）　☐ friendly（親しみやすい）　☐ cheerful（明るい／前向きな）
☐ honest（真面目）　☐ clever（賢い）　☐ diligent（勤勉な）
☐ funny（面白い）　☐ quiet（静か／おとなしい）　☐ calm（落ち着いている）
☐ talkative（よくしゃべる）

12 どんな音楽を聴く？
Music

　生徒の多くは，音楽に興味を持っています。「音楽」をテーマに Small Talk をすると，たくさん話したいことが出てくるでしょう。音楽が好きでない生徒には，What do you like? と聞いて，好きな話題で話をさせます。

文法事項	現在形 (be 動詞・一般動詞)　疑問詞 (How many, How often, Who, Whose) There is/are 構文
主な表現	Do you like music?　What kind of music do you like? What is your favorite song of BTS?　Do you like singing songs? Do you go to karaoke?　How often do you go to karaoke? Whose songs do you sing?　How many members are there in BTS? Who are they?　Who do you like?　等
実施時期	中学 1 年　11 月
留意点	Small Talk を始める前に，タブレットで自分の好きな歌手を検索させておき，写真等を見せながら，「準備のある Small Talk」も取り入れてみましょう。
応用・発展	Animation ☞ Do you watch anime?〔アニメは見る？〕 Comic Books ☞ Do you have comic books?〔漫画，持っている？〕

Teacher's Talk

T: Hello. Do you like music? When I was a junior high school student, I liked playing the guitar, and I liked singing songs of Kaguya-hime, Iruka and Matsuyama Chiharu. I often played the guitar in my free time. Do you like music?

S1: Yes. I like back number.

T: Oh, I know the name of the group. How many people are there in back number?

S1: Three.

T: Who do you like in the group?

S1: I like Shimizu Iyori.

T: Do you sing their songs at karaoke?

S1: No, I just listen to their songs.

中学1年 すらすら英会話
su ra su ra ei kai wa

Let's talk about 'Music.'

Today's Point 相手の話に肯定的に反応しましょう。

① Do you listen to music?

❶ Yes, I do.

② What kind of music do you listen?

❷ I listen to pop music.

③ Me too. Do you listen to rock music?

❸ No, I don't like rock.

④ Me neither. Who is your favorite artist?

❹ I like BTS.

⑤ What is your favorite BTS song?

❺ I like "Dynamite" the best.

⑥ How many members are there in BTS?

❻ There are 7 members.

⑦ Who are they?

❼ They are Jin, Suga, J-hope ….

⑧ Who do you like?

❽ I like Jin.

⑨ Do you like singing songs?

❾ Yes, I do. I like singing.

⑩ Same here. Do you go to karaoke?

❿ Yes, I do.

⑪ How often do you go to karaoke?

⓫ Maybe, 2 or 3 times a month.

⑫ Whose songs do you sing?

⓬ I sing songs of Ai-myon, ….

Useful Expressions 共感する表現を使ってみましょう。

☐ Me too. (私も)　　☐ Me neither. (私も～でない)　　☐ Same here. (同じく／私も)

☐ I'm with you. (同感です)　　☐ That's true. (確かに)　　☐ Sounds good. (いいね)

☐ You're right. (その通りです)　　☐ Exactly. (その通り)

47

13 好きなことは何？
Favorite Thing to Do

　好きなことをテーマに，「動名詞」を用いて Small Talk を行います。好きなことを尋ねたら，その話題で対話が続くように，様々な質問をし，話題を深めていくようにします。

文法事項	現在形（be 動詞・一般動詞）　疑問詞（What, How long）　動名詞
主な表現	What do you like doing?　What games do you like playing? How long do you play it a day? What do you like doing on weekend?　What did you do at the mall? What else do you like doing?　等
実施時期	中学 1 年　12月
留意点	対話を継続していくためには，相手の発言を「繰り返し」たり，「相づち」を打ったり，「感想」を言ったりする等の反応が大事です。同時に，話を深く掘り下げたり，話題を広げたりするような「質問」をすることを加えていくようにします。
応用・発展	Favorite Movie 　　☞ What is your favorite movie?〔お気に入りの映画は？〕 Favorite Place to Eat 　　☞ What is your favorite place to eat？〔食事はどこに行くのが好き？〕

Teacher's Talk

T : What do you like doing? As all of you know about me, I like growing vegetables. Growing vegetables is a lot of fun. I am growing Chinese cabbage, onions, garlics, cabbage now. What do you like doing, S1?

S1: I like playing soccer.

T : Yes, you like playing soccer. Who is your favorite soccer player?

S1: I like Mr. Kubo.

T : Why do you like him?

S1: His soccer skills are so great. He is good at shooting and dribbling.

T : Do you want to be like him?

S1: Yes.（他，数名に尋ねていく）

T : O.K. Let's talk about 'Favorite Thing to Do.'

48

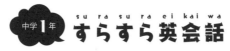

Let's talk about 'Favorite Thing to Do.'

Today's Point 様々な質問をして，相手のことを詳しく知りましょう。

① What do you like doing? ❶ I like playing video games.

② What games do you like playing? ❷ I like the ○○○ game. It's a shooting game.

③ Do you play video games every day? ❸ Yes. Playing games is fun.

④ Are you good at playing video games? ❹ Yes. I'm good at playing games.

⑤ How long do you play it a day? ❺ I play it for two hours. I enjoy playing video games. I cannot stop playing it.

⑥ What time do you go to bed? ❻ I go to bed at 11:30.

⑦ When do you study? ❼ I usually study after dinner.

⑧ What do you like doing on weekends? ❽ I like going shopping.

⑨ Did you go shopping last weekend? ❾ Yes, I went to ABC mall.

⑩ What did you do at the mall? ❿ I ate ice cream, and I bought a bag.

⑪ What else do you like doing? ⓫ I like drawing pictures. Drawing pictures is very fun.

Useful Expressions

〔対話を続ける方法〕 ①繰り返す ②相づちを打つ ③感想を言う ④質問する

☐ Are you ～?　☐ Do you ～?　☐ Did you ～?　☐ Can you ～?
☐ What ...（何）　☐ When ...（いつ）　☐ Where ...（どこで）　☐ How ...（どのように）
☐ Who ...（誰）　☐ Who ... with（誰と）　☐ Whose ...（誰の）　☐ Which ...（どっち）

14 冬休みの出来事
My Winter Vacation

　　中学1年生の3学期に過去形を学習します。お互い冬休みにやったことを伝え合い，友だちの冬休みの過ごし方を知る機会としましょう。

文法事項	現在形（一般動詞）　過去形（be 動詞・一般動詞）　疑問詞（What, When, Where, Why, Who, Who … with, How, How much）
主な表現	How was your winter vacation?　What did you do? How was it?　How much did you receive? Did you go anywhere?　Where did you go?　Why did you go there? How did you go there?　When did you go there? Who did you go with?　等
実施時期	中学1年　1月
留意点	「おみくじを引く」「おせちを食べる」「大掃除をする」等，日本の伝統文化について触れるとともに，予想される英語表現を生徒に提示しておくとよいです。
応用・発展	Last Night ☞ What did you do last night?〔昨夜，何をした？〕 Summer or Winter ☞ Which do you prefer?〔どっちが好き？〕

Teacher's Talk

T: Hi. Did you enjoy your winter vacation? We had a 15-day holiday this winter vacation. Did you go anywhere? I spent my time doing a lot of things. On New Year's Eve, my daughters' family came to my house, and we watched TV. We ate *soba*. We enjoyed talking. On January 2nd, I went to Narita Temple with my wife. I prayed for our happiness. On January 4th, my wife and I went to Chiba. We stayed at a hotel near Tokyo Disneyland. We enjoyed the dinner. The next day, we went to Tokyo Disneyland. I enjoyed "Enchanted Tale of Beauty and the Beast" and "The Happy Ride with Baymax" for the first time. I enjoyed them a lot. What did you do this winter vacation?

S1: I went to my cousin's house in Yokohama.

T: What did you do with your cousin?

S1: We went to Chinese restaurant. I ate 肉まん.

Let's talk about 'My Winter Vacation.'

Today's Point 5W1H（What, When, Where, Why, Who, How）を用いて，相手のことを詳しく知りましょう。

① How was your winter vacation?　　　❶ It was good.

② What did you do?　　　❷ I cleaned my house.
　　　　　　　　　　　　　　I ate *soba* on New Year's Eve.
　　　　　　　　　　　　　　I went to the shrine on New Year's Day. I prayed for my happiness.
　　　　　　　　　　　　　　I drew a fortune slip.

③ How was it?　　　❸ It was an excellent luck.

④ How nice! Congratulations.　　　❹ I received new year's gift.

⑤ How much did you receive?　　　❺ I received 45,000 yen in total.

⑥ Did you go anywhere?　　　❻ Yes, I did.

⑦ Where did you go?　　　❼ I went to Nagano.

⑧ Why did you go there?　　　❽ I went skiing.

⑨ How did you go there?　　　❾ I went there by car.

⑩ When did you go there?　　　❿ I went there from Jan. 2nd to Jan. 4th.

⑪ Who did you go with?　　　⓫ I went there with my family.

Useful Expressions 5W1Hを用いて，質問攻めにしましょう。

☐ What did you eat?（何を食べたの？）　　☐ Who did you go with?（誰と行ったの？）
☐ Where did you buy?（どこで買ったの？）　☐ How did you go?（どうやって行ったの？）
☐ When did you see?（いつ見たの？）　　　☐ Why did you go there?（なぜそこへ行ったの？）

15 昨夜6時頃，何していた？
Last Night

　過去のある時点で何をしていたかを尋ねる過去進行形を用いて，昨夜の行動を尋ね合います。過去形を用いるべきか，過去進行形を用いるべきか，時制に留意させましょう。

文法事項	現在形（be 動詞・一般動詞）　過去形（be 動詞・一般動詞）過去進行形　疑問詞（What, What time, How long, Why）
主な表現	What were you doing?　How long did it take to do the homework?　It took one hour.　What time did you start doing it?　How long did you play it?　I was playing online game.　等
実施時期	中学1年　2月
留意点	過去進行形は，通常，特定の日時を指し，その時刻に何をしていたのかを言い表す表現となりますが，「昨夜，何していた？」と言う時は，What were you doing last night? もしくは過去形を用いて What did you do last night? と言うことができます。
応用・発展	Yesterday 　　☞ What did you do yesterday?〔昨日，何していた？〕 Childhood 　　☞ When you were little, what were you doing?〔子供の時，何してた？〕

Teacher's Talk

T : Yesterday, I got home at 7:00. When I got home, my wife was cooking in the kitchen. I was too hungry.

T : What were you doing at 7:00 last night?　　S1: I was eating dinner.

T : You were eating dinner. What did you eat?　　S1: I ate ... 煮物.

T : What were the vegetables?　　S1: Potato, carrot, radish.

T : So, you ate simmered vegetables.
　 I was watching TV at 9:00.
　 What were you doing at 9:00 last night?
　 Do you remember?　　S2: I was studying.

T : What were you studying?　　S2: I was studying Japanese.

T : Great! How was it?　　S2: It was good.

52

Let's talk about 'Last Night.'

Today's Point 1つの話題から，対話を広げたり，深めたりしましょう。

① You look sleepy today.

② Wow, so late! What were you doing?

③ What subject was it?

④ Wow, it was a hard time. How long did it take to do the homework?

⑤ What did you say? Just one hour? What time did you start doing it?

⑥ Oh, my god! What were you doing until then?

⑦ Are you sure? How long did you play it?

⑧ Four hours? You spent four hours playing online games?

⑨ I was ... doing online games too.

⑩ I'm Ray.

❶ Yes, I went to bed at 1 am.

❷ I was doing my homework.

❸ It was a math homework. It was too difficult.

❹ Let me see. It took one hour.

❺ I started doing my homework at midnight.

❻ I was playing online games.

❼ I played it for four hours.

❽ Yes. I totally forgot to do my homework. By the way, what were you doing?

❾ What's your name?

❿ Ray? I'm Ace. Nice to see you.

Useful Expressions 様々な表現を用い，会話を続けるようにしましょう。

☐ It was a hard time.（大変だったね）　☐ Let me see.（えーと）　☐ Oh, my god!（あらま！）
☐ What did you say?（何だって？）　☐ Are you sure?（本当ですか？）
☐ By the way,（ところで）　☐ Unbelievable.（信じられない）

ひとくち英語 ① 1 ⇒ 30

① わかりました。
② 私も。
③ あなたも？
④ 私も〜でない。
⑤ うんうん。
⑥ そうなんだ？
⑦ そうなんだよ。
⑧ もう少し話して。
⑨ えーと。
⑩ いいね。
⑪ その通り。
⑫ もう一度言って。
⑬ 本当？
⑭ 素晴らしい。
⑮ 私もそう期待します。
⑯ すごいね。
⑰ そんなにたくさん！
⑱ 本当に？／マジで？
⑲ 本気です。／真面目です。
⑳ まさか！／ウソでしょ！／すごい！
㉑ ところで，
㉒ よくわからないけど…
㉓ たぶん。
㉔ そうなんだ。
㉕ そうですよね。／私もそう思います。
㉖ かわいいね！
㉗ 信じられない。
㉘ いい考えね。
㉙ やったね！
㉚ 何だって？

① I see.
② Me too. / Same here.
③ You too?
④ Me neither.
⑤ Uh-huh.
⑥ Is that right?
⑦ Right.
⑧ Tell me more.
⑨ Well ..., / Let's see, ... / Let me see.
⑩ Great. / Nice. / Good. / Sounds good.
⑪ That's right. / Exactly.
⑫ Pardon? / Pardon me?
⑬ Really? / Are you sure?
⑭ Cool. / Fabulous.
⑮ I hope so too.
⑯ Amazing. / Awesome. / Great.
⑰ So many!
⑱ Are you serious? / Really?
⑲ I'm serious.
⑳ No way!
㉑ By the way,
㉒ I'm not sure, but ....
㉓ Maybe.
㉔ Is that so?
㉕ I feel the same. / I'm with you.
㉖ Cute!
㉗ Unbelievable.
㉘ Nice idea.
㉙ You did it. / Well done.
㉚ What did you say?

中学2年で扱いたい！
トピック別
「すらすら英会話」
15

1 お互いを知ろう①
Get to know each other

　2年生に進級し，クラス替え等で，今まであまり話したことのない友だちや，初めて会う友だちがいるかも知れません。ビジネスにおける Small Talk は，その後の交渉がうまくいくように，お互いを知り合うという目的で行います。それと同様に，英語授業においても，友だちとの協働的な学習が可能となるよう，人間関係づくりに Small Talk を行いたいです。1年生で学習した英語の復習を兼ね，お互いを知る Small Talk から始めましょう。

| 文法事項 | 現在形・過去形（be 動詞・一般動詞）　現在進行形　動名詞 |

| 主な表現 | Nice to see you.　How was your class?　It was fun.
I enjoyed it very much.　Are you practicing the piano?
What do you like doing?　When did you start playing it?
Why did you start playing it?　What else do you like doing?　等 |

| 実施時期 | 中学2年　4月中旬 |

| 留意点 | Nice to meet you. は初めて会った時に使い，「また会えたね」では，Nice to see you. と see を使います。発展的な活動として，隣の生徒と Small Talk をした後，前後でペアにさせ，隣の生徒を紹介させると，必然的に3人称単数現在形を用いる活動となり，1年生のよい復習となります。 |

| 応用・発展 | Dreams for This School Year
　👉 What do you want to do this year?〔今年の夢は？〕
What You Do on Holidays
　👉 What do you do on holidays?〔休みはどう過ごす？〕 |

Teacher's Talk

T : Hello, everyone. I think you know my name. What is my name? (Ss: Mr.Takizawa.)
Yes. My name is Hiroto Takizawa. Do you know where I am from? (Ss: Saitama?)
No, I am from Tokyo. I'm 58 years old. This is my granddaughter. (写真) I am a grandpa. When I have free time, I like growing vegetables, reading books, going to hot springs and watching TV. What do you like doing?　S1: I like playing soccer.

T : Who is your favorite soccer player?　　　　　　　S1: Mr. Kubo.

T : What is your position?　　　　　　　　　　　　　S1: I am a midfielder.

Get to know each other.

Today's Point 積極的に質問して，友だちのことをよく知りましょう。

① Hello. How are you?

② Terrific! Nice to see you.

③ You were in class 1-B, right?

④ I was in 1-A. How was your class?

⑤ It was fun. I enjoyed it very much. Are you practicing the piano?

⑥ What do you like doing?

⑦ Do you like singing songs?

⑧ When did you start playing it?

⑨ Why did you start playing it?

⑩ What else do you like doing?

⑪ Wow, I look forward to your cookies. I love cookies.

❶ I'm good. How are you?

❷ Nice to see you again.

❸ Yes. Which class were you in?

❹ It was great. How about you?

❺ Yes, I am. I practice the piano every day.

❻ Guess what?

❼ Yes, but I am poor at singing. I like playing the piano.

❽ I started playing it when I was 3.

❾ My sister was learning the piano. So, I wanted to learn it.

❿ I like making cookies.

⓫ What did you say?

Tips!
たくさん質問して，Small Talk が終わったら，今度は前後でペアになり，隣の友だちのことを伝え合ってみましょう。

2 ゴールデンウィークには何する？
Your Plans for Golden Week

　Small Talk は，できるだけタイムリーな話題が望ましいです。生徒は未来形を学習する頃ですので，これからのことを話題にする Small Talk を行いましょう。

文法事項	未来形 (be going to / will)　疑問詞 (What, Where, When, How long)
主な表現	Do you have plans for Golden Week?　What are your plans? Where are you going?　Who are you going with?　When are you going? How long are you going to stay?　What are you going to do? What else will you do?　Will you have tennis practice? What team will you play against?　等
実施時期	中学2年　4月下旬
留意点	5W1H を使って，たくさん質問できる力を付けたいです。使った疑問詞には，□に✓を入れるなど Small Talk シートに入れておくとよいでしょう。
応用・発展	This Weekend 　　☞ What are you going to do this weekend?〔今週末の予定は何？〕 Tonight 　　☞ What will you do tonight?〔今夜は何をする？〕

Teacher's Talk

T : We'll have public holidays next week. Do you have plans for the holidays? I'm going somewhere with my wife on May 3rd because it is her birthday. I'm going to celebrate her birthday. May 5th is our wedding anniversary. I have no ideas where to go, but we'll go somewhere and eat dinner.

T : What are your plans?　　　　　　　S1: I'm going to a Saucy Dog concert.

T : Oh, did you buy the ticket?　　　　　S1: Yes, I did.

T : Where are you going?　　　　　　　S1: I'm going to Yokohama arena.

T : Wow, who are you going with?　　　S1: I'm going with Yuki and Hiro.
　　　　　　　　　　　　　　　　　　　　　　　We're going on May 4th.

T : Enjoy the concert! How about S2?　　S2: I have no plans.

T : Oh, you have no plans?
　　Will you have tennis practice?　　　S2: Yes, maybe.

中学2年 すらすら英会話
su ra su ra ei kai wa

Let's talk about 'Plans for Golden Week.'

Today's Point 5W1H (What, When, Where, Why, Who, How) を用いて，質問しましょう。

① Do you have plans for Golden Week? ❶ Yes, I do.

② What are your plans? ❷ I'm going camping.

③ Where are you going? ❸ I'm going to Tochigi.

④ Who are you going with? ❹ I'm going with my family.

⑤ When are you going? ❺ We are going on May 2nd.

⑥ How long are you going to stay? ❻ We're going to stay for two nights.

⑦ What are you going to do at the camp? ❼ We are going to cook curry.

⑧ How will the weather be during GW? ❽ I'm not sure, but it'll be sunny.

⑨ What else will you do during GW? ❾ I have no plans.

⑩ Will you have tennis practice? ❿ Yes! We'll have a tennis match.

⑪ When are you going to have it? ⓫ I forgot. Maybe, on May 5th.

⑫ What team will you play against? ⓬ We will play against Kita JHS.

⑬ Kita JHS? I'll go and cheer you on. ⓭ No way! Please do not come!

Useful Expressions 終わりの言葉を工夫して伝えましょう。

☐ Thank you for talking with me. （私と話してくれてありがとう）

☐ You speak English very well. （英語がとても上手ですね）

☐ It was great talking with you. （あなたと話ができてとてもよかったよ）

59

3 ゴールデンウィークはどう過ごした？
Memories of Golden Week

　楽しみにしていたゴールデンウィークも終わってしまいました。生徒はどんな休みを過ごしたのでしょうか。ゴールデンウィークをどう過ごしたのか振り返らせましょう。

| 文法事項 | 過去形（be 動詞・一般動詞）　不定詞（副詞的用法） |

| 主な表現 | How were your holidays?　How did you spend the holidays? |

Where did you go shopping?　What did you buy?　How was it?

Did you have baseball games?　Why did you go to Nikko?

I went to Nikko to see my aunt.　Did you stay there?　等

| 実施時期 | 中学2年　5月中旬 |

| 留意点 | 質問されて答えるだけでなく，それに関して付け足しの文を言うことを習慣にします。2年生では，質問に答えたら，複数の文をつなげて答えられる力を付けていきたいです。matching caps は，おそろいの帽子という意味です。 |

| 応用・発展 | Last Weekend |

　　☞ How did you spend last weekend?〔先週末はどう過ごしたの？〕

Holiday

　　☞ What do you do on your holiday?〔休みには何をする？〕

Teacher's Talk

T: Wow, our holidays are over. Did you enjoy the holidays? I enjoyed them. As I told you, May 3rd is my wife's birthday, so we went on a day trip to Lake Haruna. We ate sandwiches and drank coffee. I made sandwiches for her.（写真）We rode on a boat too.（写真）On the way back home, we ate dinner at a restaurant. I gave her a birthday present.（写真）May 5th is our wedding anniversary. My daughters came to my house and had a barbeque. We had tennis matches against Kita JHS. We won the matches.

T: How did you spend your holidays?　　S1: I went camping.

T: Tell me more.　　　　　　　　　　　　S1: I went camping ... in Yamanashi.
　　　　　　　　　　　　　　　　　　　　　　I stayed there for one night.

T: Do you have any questions for S1?　S2: What did you do there?
　　　　　　　　　　　　　　　　　　　　　　S1: I cooked and ate curry.

60

中学2年 すらすら英会話

Let's talk about 'How we spent Golden Week.'

Today's Point 相手の言ったことに，積極的に「反応」しながら Small Talk をしましょう。

① How were your holidays?

❶ Great. I enjoyed them a lot.

② How did you spend the holidays?

❷ I spent the holidays having a barbeque, going shopping, playing baseball, and traveling to Nikko.

③ You enjoyed the holidays too. Where did you go shopping?

❸ I went to ABC mall in Tokyo with my friends. It was so crowded.

④ What did you buy?

❹ I bought a nice and cheap shirt. We bought matching caps too.

⑤ Nice. How was the barbeque?

❺ It was fun. I had a barbeque with my grandparents by the river.

⑥ How was the weather?

❻ It was sunny. It was a hot day.

⑦ Did you play baseball games?

❼ Yes. We played against Nishi JHS.

⑧ How was it?

❽ We won two games, but we lost one.

⑨ Why did you go to Nikko?

❾ I went there to see my aunt.

⑩ Did you stay there?

❿ No, it was a day trip.

⑪ Do you miss Golden Week?

⓫ Of course ..., and I missed you.

Useful Expressions 反応の表現を使いながら，会話を2分間，続けてみましょう。

①繰り返す　　　(Tokyo? / You went to Tokyo?) ⤴相手の言ったことの一部や文を繰り返す。

②相づちを打つ　(I see. / Really? / Me too. / I didn't know that.) ⤴話に合わせる。

③質問する　　　(What did you buy? / How was it?) ⤴深く尋ねたり，話題を広げたりする。

④感想を言う　　(Nice. I like it. / I think so too.) ⤴自分の考えや気持ちを伝える。

61

4 お気に入りのレストランは？
My Favorite Restaurant

　生徒たちは，どんなレストランに行くのでしょうか。お気に入りのレストランについて，Small Talk を行わせ，生徒理解を深めましょう。タブレットを用いて，店の写真や料理の写真，メニュー等を見せ合いながら，時には，準備のある Small Talk もよいでしょう。

文法事項	不定詞（副詞的用法）　接続詞 (if, when)

主な表現	Where do you like to eat when you go out?
	What do you like to eat there?　How much is the hamburger steak?
	Where is the restaurant?
	How long does it take from here to the restaurant?
	How far is it from here?　Where do you go if you want to eat *ramen*?
	What do you recommend?　How much is that?　等

実施時期	中学2年　6月

留意点	What do you recommend? の質問に対して，気を付けたい点は，I recommend strawberry cake. のように目的語がくるところです。もし「あなたに勧める」という時は，I recommend you to ... とは言わず，I recommend that you should eat strawberry cake. のように，that 節を用います。

応用・発展	Fast Food
	☞ What's your favorite fast food?〔好きなファーストフードは？〕
	Shopping ☞ Where do you often go shopping?〔買い物はどこに行く？〕

Teacher's Talk

T: This is my favorite restaurant.（写真）It's G-Restaurant. The meals are very cheap. We can choose from many different drinks, and they have an outlet so I can use my computer and work there. When I want to eat *ramen*, I like to go to Dosanko *ramen*. Its *miso-ramen* is delicious.

T: What is your favorite restaurant?　　S1: I go to M-Italian restaurant.

T: What do you like to eat?　　S1: I like pasta. It is delicious.

T: Where is the restaurant?　　S1: It's in Nagoya.

T: Wow, do you go there by car?　　S1: Yes. I go with my family.

T: O.K. Today, let's use a tablet. Show some pictures and have a chat.

中学**2**年 **su ra su ra ei kai wa すらすら英会話**

Let's talk about 'My Favorite Restaurant.'

Today's Point 答えたら1，2文付け足し，詳しく話すようにしましょう。

① Where do you like to eat when you go out?

❶ I like to go to ABC restaurant. It's an Italian restaurant.

② What do you like to eat there?

❷ I like to eat the hamburger steak. Its hamburger steak is my favorite dish. It's hot and juicy.

③ How much is it?

❸ It's 800 yen. It's cheap and tasty.

④ Sounds good. Where is the restaurant?

❹ It's near the post office.

⑤ How long does it take from here to the restaurant?

❺ It takes about 10 minutes by car. My brother drives me there.

⑥ How far is it from here?

❻ It's about 5 kilometers.

⑦ Where do you usually go when you eat *ramen*?

❼ I often go to ABC *ramen* shop. Its *ramen* is so delicious.

⑧ What do you recommend?

❽ I recommend the *miso-ramen*.

⑨ How much is that?

❾ It's 660 yen.

⑩ Wow, so cheap. If you are free tomorrow, let's go to eat *ramen*!

❿ What did you say? Please go alone.

Useful Expressions

☐ How long does it take from A to B? (AからBはどのくらい時間がかかりますか？)

☐ How far is it from here? (ここからどのくらい距離がありますか？)

☐ What are you talking about? (何言っているの？)

63

5 今夜の予定は？
Plans for Tonight

　中学生は帰宅後，どんな生活を送っているのでしょうか。未来形とともに，must や have to, must not, don't have to などを用いて，家庭内ルールも話していきましょう。

文法事項	未来形 (be going to / will)

　　　　　　助動詞 (must, must not, have to, don't have to)　構文 (It is ... for ... to 〜)

主な表現	What are you going to do tonight?　What time will you go to *juku*?

　　　　　　When will you have dinner?　What are you going to study at *juku*?

　　　　　　How long do you study at *juku*?

　　　　　　What time do you have to get up tommorow?　等

実施時期	中学2年　6月下旬

留意点	自分の意志でやらなくてはいけないと思うことは，must を用い，周りの状況から，そうしなくてはいけない場合は，have to を用いることなど，実際のコミュニケーションの中で，活用の仕方を身に付けさせていきます。

応用・発展	School Rules

　　　　☞What school rules are not necessary?〔不要な校則は？〕

　　　Family Rules

　　　　☞What are your family rules?〔家庭内ルールは？〕

Teacher's Talk

T : What are you going to do after school? I will get home around 7 o'clock.
　 I will take a bath, and I will have dinner. I must cook dinner. Maybe, I will eat
　 grilled fish and *tofu*. After dinner, I must do some work. I must finish a report
　 by next week. I will go to bed at 11:30.

T : What are your plans for tonight?　　　S1: I will watch YouTube.

T : What will you watch?　　　　　　　　S1: I will watch Hikakin's YouTube.

T : Is he your favorite YouTuber?　　　　S1: Yes, I like him.

T : What do you have to do tonight?　　　S2: I must go to judo practice.

T : What time will the practice begin?　　S2: It will start at 7:00.

T : So, what time do you have to get home? S2: I must get home by 6:30.

T : When will you have dinner?　　　　　S2: I'll have dinner after the practice.

Let's talk about 'Plans for Tonight.'

Today's Point 様々な質問をして，話題を広げましょう。

① What are you going to do tonight?
❶ Tonight? I must go to *juku*.

② What time will you go to *juku*?
❷ I will go to *juku* at 6:30.

③ What time do you have to get home?
❸ I must get home by 6:00.

④ When will you have dinner?
❹ I have no time to eat dinner before *juku*, so I will eat after *juku*.

⑤ What are you going to study at *juku*?
❺ I'm going to study math.

⑥ How long do you study at *juku*?
❻ I study for two hours.

⑦ What do you have to do tonight?
❼ Well, I must study for the math test.

⑧ What time will you go to bed?
❽ I will go to bed at midnight.

⑨ What time do you have to get up tomorrow?
❾ I must get up at 6:00. I must walk my dog every morning.

⑩ Is it easy for you to get up early?
❿ Yes. I can get up early easily. It is fun for me to walk my dog.

⑪ What time is it?
⓫ It's 6:10. Oh, I must go home. I'll be late for *juku*!!!

Useful Expressions

☐ I must get home <u>by 6:00</u>.（6時までには家に帰らなくてはいけないんです）
☐ Do you <u>have to</u> study at home too?（家でも勉強しなくてはいけないの？）
☐ <u>It is fun</u> <u>for</u> me <u>to</u> walk my dogs.（犬の散歩は，楽しいです）

65

6 夏祭りには行くの？
Summer Festival

　中学生にとって楽しい行事の１つは，夏祭りでしょう。夏祭りに行くと，友だちに会えたり，色々食べられたり，花火を見たり，涼んだり…。夏休み前の話題にしたいです。

文法事項	未来形(be going to / will)　接続詞(when)　過去形　助動詞(must, must not, have to, don't have to)　構文(It is ... for ... to ～)　不定詞(名詞的用法)
主な表現	Are you going to a summer festival? Did you go to a summer festival last year?　Was it crowded? Do you wear a *yukata* when you go to festivals? What do you like to eat?　What flavor do you like?　等
実施時期	中学２年　７月
留意点	地域によっては，お祭りに参加する生徒が多いと思います。そんな時は，I join the festival. I play the drum. Adults are kind to us. などと言ってくる生徒がいることでしょう。どんなことをするのか，尋ねたいです。
応用・発展	Summer Vacation 　👉 What's your plan for summer vacation?〔夏休みの予定は？〕 Favorite Place 　👉 Where do you like going in summer?〔夏にどこに行くのが好き？〕

Teacher's Talk

T : Summer Festival in our town will be held on July 28th. Are you going to the festival? I'm going there. I go to the festival every year. I enjoy eating some food from the food stall. I like to eat *takoyaki* and *yakisoba*. Shaved ice is delicious too. I like strawberry flavor.

T : Are you going to a summer festival?　　　　S1: Yes, I am.

T : What do you do at the festival?　　　　　　S1: I play the drum.

T : Oh, do you join the festival?　　　　　　　S1: Yes, I do.

T : How about you, S2? Are you going this year?　S2: Maybe. I will go.

T : When you go to the festival, what do you do?　S2: I eat *kaki-gori*.

T : Oh, you eat shaved ice. What flavor do you like?　S2: I like lemon flavor.

Let's talk about 'Summer Festival.'

Today's Point 相手の目をしっかり見て，会話しましょう。

① Are you going to a summer festival?

❶ Of course, I am.

② Did you go to a summer festival last year?

❷ Yes, I did. I went to the Sumida River Fireworks Festival.

③ Wow, nice! Was it crowded?

❸ Yes, it was. Many people were there.

④ Do you wear a *yukata* when you go to festivals?

❹ No. I don't have a *yukata*. I wear casual clothes.

⑤ What do you like to eat at festivals?

❺ I like to eat shaved ice.

⑥ What flavor do you like?

❻ I like blue Hawaii or strawberry.

⑦ Do you eat *takoyaki*?

❼ Yes. I love it. It's easy to eat.

⑧ I think so too.
What do you like about festivals?

❽ It is fun for me to buy some food at food stalls, talk with my friends, and watch fireworks.

⑨ What time do you have to go home?

❾ I must be home by 10. That is our family rule.

⑩ Good! It is important for us to follow the family rules.

❿ I think so too. What's yours?

Useful Expressions

☐ Of course.（もちろん）　　☐ Was it crowded?（混んでいた？）
☐ It's easy to eat.（食べやすい）　☐ What flavor do you like?（何味が好き？）
☐ What do you like about festivals?（お祭りのどんなところが好きなの？）
☐ I think so too.（私もそう思う）

7 私たちの町はどんな町？
Our Town

　生徒は，小学校の英語授業で私の町の紹介を伝え合います。同じテーマを用い，中学生もやってみると面白いでしょう。中学英語ならではの There is/are 構文や，不定詞（There are many places to visit.）などが使えます。自分の住んでいる町を誇りに思う生徒を育てたいものです。

文法事項	There is/are 構文　不定詞（形容詞的用法）

主な表現	Where do you live?　Where in Saitama do you live? What do you have in Chichibu?　What do you like about your town? What is your town famous for?　Are there any good places to visit?　等

実施時期	中学2年　9月

留意点	「～があります」で注意点は，固有名詞には，There is/are を用いないということです。We have や They have を用います。また，「～がありません」では，一般的に多く存在するものは，There are no 名詞の複数形（There are not 名詞の複数形）．を使い，通常は1つ程度の場合，There is no 名詞の単数形（There is not a 名詞の単数形）．を用いる等，実際のコミュニケーションにおいて活用できる技能となるように指導します。

応用・発展	My Prefecture 　↳ What can you do in your prefecture?〔都道府県の見どころ〕 Favorite Amusement Park 　↳ What is your favorite amusement park?〔お気に入りの遊園地〕

Teacher's Talk

T : Hello, what do you like about your town? I like my town. I like living in the countryside. I like a quiet place. I like to see beautiful stars at night. You can see many wild animals, such as monkeys, deer, and wild boars.

T : What do you have in your town?　　　　　S1: We have a big shopping mall.

T : Oh, nice. What is the name of the mall?　S1: ABC mall.

T : Yes, it is big. What do you like?　　　　　S2: I like the library.

T : Why?　　　　　　　　　　　　　　　　　S2: I can borrow books and DVDs.

T : How often do you go to the library?　　　S2: Every weekend.

Let's talk about 'Our Town.'

Today's Point 質問に答えたら，文を付け足し，詳しく話すようにしましょう。

① Where do you live?
❶ I live in Saitama.

② Where in Saitama do you live?
❷ I live in Chichibu.

③ What do you have in Chichibu?
❸ We have mountains and rivers.
There are many wild animals too.
It is rich in nature.

④ What do you like about your town?
❹ First, air and water are clean.
Second, the food is delicious.
Third, people are kind and friendly.

⑤ What is your town famous for?
❺ My town is famous for its *soba*.
Fruit is also famous in my town.
There is a lot of delicious food too.

⑥ Are there any good places to visit?
❻ Yes. There are many places to visit.

⑦ What is a good place to visit?
❼ We have shrines.
We have Hitsuji-yama Park too.
You can see shiba-zakura in spring.

⑧ What do you want in your town?
❽ I want a big library and a museum.

⑨ Do you want a zoo?
❾ That's O.K. I can see many wild animals near my house.

Useful Expressions

☐ <u>Where in Saitama</u> do you live? （埼玉のどこに住んでいるの？）
☐ <u>Are there any good places to</u> visit? （どこか行くところ，<u>よいところある</u>？）
☐ <u>There is no</u> museum, no zoo .... （美術館とか動物園は<u>ないね</u>）

69

8 お気に入りのテレビ番組は？
My Favorite TV Program

　生徒の身近な生活に，テレビや YouTube があります。10月には，テレビの秋の新番組が始まりますので，Small Talk の話題にはちょうどよいでしょう。番組の内容を少しでも伝えられるように，表現を増やし，説明することに慣れさせていきましょう。

文法事項	現在形（be 動詞・一般動詞）　動名詞
主な表現	Do you like watching TV?　What kind of TV shows do you watch? What TV dramas are you watching? Who appears in the drama?　Who is the main character? What is the story about?　How long is the TV drama? When is it on TV?　What's on TV tonight?　等
実施時期	中学２年　10月上旬
留意点	２年生の後半に入ります。徐々に「説明力」を付けさせていきます。What's that?（それは何？）や，What is the story about?（どんな話なの？）という質問をし，それに複数の文で説明できるようにさせていきたいです。ただ，Small Talk はあくまでも既習事項の定着にありますので，それらの学習は，授業の中で，集中的に指導していくとよいでしょう。
応用・発展	YouTube ☞ Who is your favorite YouTuber?〔好きなユーチューバーは？〕 Favorite Movie ☞ What kind of movies do you like?〔どんな映画が好き？〕

Teacher's Talk

T : What do you like to do at home? I like to do two things. First, I like sleeping. When I am tired or I have nothing to do, I soon go to bed and sleep. Second, I like watching TV. My favorite TV drama is a detective one. I like watching it.

T : What TV shows do you like to watch?　　　　S1: I like music ....

T : Oh, you like music shows.
　　What is the name of the show?　　　　　　　S1: It's Music Station.

T : Is Mr. Tamori the MC?　　　　　　　　　　　S1: Yes.

T : Who is your favorite singer or band?　　　　　S1: I like Ai-myon.

T : What is your favorite song?　　　　　　　　　S1: I like "Marigold."

Let's talk about 'My Favorite TV Program.'

Today's Point うまく伝わらなかったら，別の言い方で言えるか考えましょう。

① Do you like watching TV?　　　　　① Yes. I like watching YouTube too.

② What kind of TV shows do you watch?　② I like to watch dramas.

③ What TV dramas are you watching?　③ I'm watching Aibo.

④ Who appears in the drama?　　　　④ Who ... appears?

⑤ <u>Who is the main character?</u>　　　⑤ Oh! Mizutani Yutaka is the main character. He is a police officer. His *aibo* ..., partner is Terawaki Yasufumi.

⑥ What is the story about?　　　　　⑥ They arrest bad people and solve crimes.

⑦ How long is the drama?　　　　　⑦ It is one hour drama.

⑧ When is it on TV?　　　　　　　　⑧ Every Wednesday.

⑨ What's on TV tonight?　　　　　　⑨ There is a movie at 9 o'clock.

⑩ What movie is it?　　　　　　　　⑩ It's a Disney movie. Its title is "Tangled." It is "塔の上のラプンツェル" in Japanese.

Useful Expressions テレビ番組の種類を使い分けましょう。

☐ ドラマ（TV drama）　☐ お笑い（comedy show）　☐ バラエティ（variety show）
☐ 刑事ドラマ（detective/crime drama）　☐ 医療ドラマ（medical TV drama）
☐ トーク番組（talk show）　☐ 音楽番組（music show）　☐ 恋愛ドラマ（romance drama）

9 お気に入りの遊園地は？
My Favorite Amusement Park

　遊園地も，生徒が話題にしやすいトピックかと思います。ディズニーリゾート，USJ，ナガシマスパーランド，富士急ハイランド，ハウステンボス，ジブリパークなどタブレットで実際のパンフレットを見ながら Small Talk をさせるとよいでしょう。

文法事項	現在形（be 動詞・一般動詞）　動名詞
主な表現	What amusement parks do you like?
	Which do you prefer, Disneyland or DisneySea?
	Do you enjoy riding on roller coasters?
	Oh, you don't like scary rides?—No.（はい）
	What do you want to ride on?
	When was the last time you went to Disneyland?　等
実施時期	中学2年　10月下旬
留意点	生徒に教えておきたい表現として，否定の形で質問された時の返答方法です。「怖い乗り物は好きじゃないんだ？」（You don't like scary rides.）と問われた時，「はい。好きじゃないんです」で答えるには，日本語に反して，No（, I don't）. と言うことです。生徒が自然と返答できるまで，辛抱強く指導しましょう。
応用・発展	Shopping
	☞ Where do you like to go shopping?〔どこで買い物するのが好き？〕
	My Favorite Fast Food
	☞ Do you eat fast food?〔ファーストフードは食べる？〕

Teacher's Talk

T : Do you like amusement parks? I love amusement parks. I like to ride on roller coasters. They are scary, but I enjoy them. I have been to Nagashima Spa Land. There are many scary roller coasters. Do you like scary rides?（Ss: Yes. / No.）

T : What amusement parks do you like to go?　　S1: USJ.

T : What rides do you enjoy?　　S1: "Space Fantasy-The Ride."

T : Is it scary?　　S1: No. It is fun.

T :（パンフレットを見せて）Wow, There are many rides. Let's talk!

72

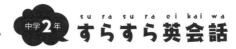

Let's talk about 'My Favorite Amusement Park.'

Today's Point 否定形で質問された時の答え方に注意しましょう。

① Do you like going to amusement parks?
❶ Yes, I love to go.

② What amusement parks do you like?
❷ Of course, I like Tokyo Disney Resort.

③ Which do you prefer, Disneyland or DisneySea?
❸ I prefer Disneyland to DisneySea. But I like both.

④ What do you enjoy at Disneyland?
❹ I enjoy watching parades. I like their dances and music.

⑤ Do you enjoy riding on roller coasters?
❺ No, I don't. They are scary.

⑥ Are you afraid of scary rides?
❻ Yes.

⑦ Oh, you don't like scary rides?
❼ No.

⑧ What do you want to ride on?
❽ Well, there are many favorite rides. But I like "Pooh's Hunny Hunt." I like Fantasy land. It's cute.

⑨ I have never been to Disneyland. When was the last time you went to Disneyland?
❾ I don't remember, but I think it was when I was a fourth grader.

⑩ O.K. Let's go to an amusement park someday.
❿ Please go alone.

Useful Expressions 遊園地のアトラクション(ride / attraction)を英語で言いましょう。

☐ ジェットコースター (roller coaster)   ☐ ティーカップ (tea cup ride)

☐ 観覧車 (Ferris wheel)   ☐ ゴーカート (go-kart)   ☐ お化け屋敷 (haunted house)

☐ バイキング (pirate ship ride)   ☐ 空中ブランコ (swing ride)

73

10 最近どう？
What's new?

What's new?（調子はどう？）は，どこかで扱いたい Small Talk の出だしの一言です。
How are you? や How's it going? と同じように用いられ，親しい間柄で交わされます。

文法事項	現在形（be 動詞・一般動詞）　動名詞

主な表現	What's new?　How's your baseball team?
	Which team did you play against?　How many games did you play?
	Did you win the games?　Did you get some hits?
	I didn't play in the games.　I am still a sub.
	Who is the best player?　How good is he?
	He is a two-way player like Mr. Otani, right?
	Do you want to be like him?　等

実施時期	中学2年　11月上旬

留意点	What's new? は，挨拶表現の一部として，「最近どう？」「何している？」「何か新しいことがあった？」ということを聞いています。これに対して，最近の出来事を話したりします。ALT がいる時に，導入するとよいでしょう。特に何もなければ，Nothing special. や Nothing much. と返答し，以前と近況が変わっていなければ，Same old. も使えます。

応用・発展	Your Life ⇨ How's life?〔最近どう？〕
	What are you up to? ⇨ What are you up to tonight?〔今夜，何する？〕

Teacher's Talk

T : Good morning. What's new, Mike?

ALT: Last Sunday was a sunny day. My wife and I took my granddaughter to a park, and we ate lunch there. We played in the park. I ran with her. After that, we went home and ate dinner. That was a fantastic day. What's new?

T : Well, I went to a hot spring in Gunma last Saturday. It was so relaxing. I had a good time. How about you? What's new?

S1: I had a judo match. ... I won the match and won first place.

T : Congratulations! Did you get the medal?

中学2年 すらすら英会話

What's new?

Today's Point 話題を見つけ，最近の出来事を語りましょう。

① What's new?

❶ Same as usual.
What's new with you?

② Pretty good.
How's your baseball team?

❷ We are practicing very hard.
We had games last Sunday.

③ Which team did you play against?

❸ We played against Nishi JHS.

④ How many games did you play?

❹ We played two games.

⑤ Did you win the games?

❺ Yes, we did.

⑥ Did you get some hits?

❻ No. I didn't play in the games.
I am still a sub.

⑦ I see. Who is the best player?

❼ Mr. Suzuki is the best.

⑧ How good is he?

❽ He is a pitcher, and he throws fastballs.
He is good at hitting too.

⑨ He is a two-way player like Mr. Otani, right?

❾ Yes, he is. He can run fast too.

⑩ Do you want to be like him?

❿ Yes. I want to be like him.

Useful Expressions 野球で使われる表現を知りましょう。

□ヒットを打つ (get a hit)　　□一塁打・二塁打を打つ (get/hit a single・a double)

□3回の表／裏 (in the top/bottom of the third winning)

□逆転する (make a comeback)　□ホームランを打つ (hit a homerun)

11 好きな季節はいつ？
Season

　暑い夏から涼しい季節になった頃，季節を話題にしてはどうでしょうか。どの季節が好きか，なぜ好きなのかを伝え合い，日本の季節のよさを伝え合わせましょう。

文法事項	現在形（be動詞・一般動詞）　疑問詞（What, When, How long, Why）
主な表現	Do you like fall?　What do you like about fall?　Autumn leaves are beautiful. What is your second favorite season?　Why do you like summer? How long is the vacation?　When does summer vacation start? When does summer vacation end?　Why not?　等
実施時期	中学2年　11月中旬
留意点	季節と言えば，四季を思い浮かべます。しかし，東南アジアなどの熱帯地方には，雨季（rainy season）と乾季（dry season）の2つしかない国もあります。日本の常識が，世界では常識となっていないことに気付かせましょう。ALTの出身国の季節について尋ね，各季節のよさを知らせ，その後，日本の四季のそれぞれのよさに気付けるようにしたいです。
応用・発展	Days of the Week 　☞ What days of the week do you like?〔好きな曜日は？〕 Favorite Month 　☞ What month is your favorite?〔何月が好き？〕

Teacher's Talk

T: It's getting cool. What season do you like? (Ss: summer/winter/fall)

T: Do you like fall? My favorite season is summer. It is humid, but I have a long vacation. What season do you like the best?　　S1: I like fall.

T: You like fall? Why?　　S1: Because it is cool.

T: Anything else?　　S1: The air is clear.

T: Yes, the air is clear. How about you, S2?　　S2: I like winter.

T: Why?　　S2: Because we have Christmas.

T: Yes! You have New Year's Day too.
　You receive New Year's gift.
　Today, we're going to talk about 'Seasons.' Make pairs.

Let's talk about 'Season.'

Today's Point 伝えたいことを整理して，伝えるようにしましょう。

① Fall is here. Do you like fall?

① Yes, fall is my favorite season.

② What do you like about fall?

② It is cool and comfortable.
Food is delicious.
Autumn leaves are beautiful.
It is a good season for a hike.

③ Do you like spring?

③ No, I don't.

④ Why not? It's a nice season.

④ Yes! I think it is a nice season, but I have a pollen allergy.
It is a hard season for me.
I hate spring.

⑤ What is your second favorite season?

⑤ Summer is my second favorite.

⑥ Really? It is too humid in summer. Why do you like summer?

⑥ Because I have a long vacation.

⑦ How long is the vacation?

⑦ We have it for about a month.

⑧ When does the summer vacation start?

⑧ It starts the end of July.

⑨ When does the summer vacation end?

⑨ It ends around August 25th.
Now, I remember. I hate summer because I have a lot of homework.

Useful Expressions

☐ Autumn leaves are beautiful.（紅葉がきれい）　☐ Why not ～?（なぜ～じゃないの？）
☐ What is your second favorite season?（２番目に好きな季節は何ですか？）
☐ I hate spring.（春は嫌いです）　☐ It is too humid in summer.（夏は蒸し暑い）

12 クリスマスはどう過ごすの？
Christmas

　1年の中でも，クリスマスは誰もが楽しみにしている行事でしょう。日本と外国のクリスマスの過ごし方の違いや，英語圏のクリスマス文化の認識を深める機会としましょう。

文法事項	未来形（be going to / will）
主な表現	Christmas season is coming soon.　Do you enjoy Christmas?
	What do you do for Christmas?
	What are you going to buy this year?
	How do you usually spend Christmas?
	How will you spend this Christmas?　等
実施時期	中学2年　12月
留意点	北米では，クリスマスに七面鳥を食べます。なぜ食べるようになったのでしょうか。諸説ありますが，イギリスの移民がアメリカに移住した頃，作物がうまく育たず，先住民に作物の育て方を教えてもらいました。すると翌年，作物が実り，飢えをしのぐことができました。その感謝祭の際に出されたのが，七面鳥でした。七面鳥料理はその後，お祝いの日の定番料理となり，クリスマスに食べるようになりました。行事の文化的背景も伝えていくとよいでしょう。
応用・発展	New Year ☞ What do you usually spend New Year?〔新年の過ごし方は？〕
	Halloween ☞ Do you enjoy Halloween?〔ハロウィンは楽しむ？〕

Teacher's Talk

T : Christmas season is coming soon. What do they eat at Christmas?（Ss: Turkey.）　Yes, but why do they eat turkey at Christmas?
Long ago, people moved from England to America. They couldn't grow vegetables well. Then, Native American showed them how to grow vegetables. The next year, they could happily get vegetables. They invited Native American and held a party. They served turkey at the table. It was the beginning for Thanksgiving Day. When they celebrate something, they began to eat turkey.

T : What are you going to eat at Christmas?　　　S1: I am going to eat cake.

T : Yes. What do you want for this Christmas?　　S2: I want games.

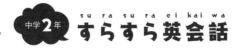

Let's talk about 'Christmas.'

Today's Point 質問に対して，できるだけ詳しく答えるようにしましょう。

① Christmas season is coming soon. Do you enjoy Christmas?

❶ Yes! I like Christmas.

② What do you do for Christmas?

❷ I go shopping and buy presents.

③ Who do you buy presents for?

❸ I buy presents for my family and friends.

④ What are you going to buy this year?

❹ I have no idea, but …, I will buy gloves for my brother.

⑤ How do you usually spend Christmas?

❺ We eat cake and chicken. We exchange presents. We enjoy talking.

⑥ Do you have a Christmas tree?

❻ Yes. We have a big Christmas tree. We put presents under the tree.

⑦ What Christmas songs do you like?

❼ I like "Mommy kissing Santa Claus" and "Santa Claus coming to town."

⑧ How will you spend this Christmas?

❽ We are planning to go to Disneyland.

⑨ How fantastic! What present do you want this year?

❾ Of course, money!

Useful Expressions

☐ Of course.（もちろん）
☐ I have no idea, but ….（わかりませんが…）
☐ Who do you buy presents for?（誰にプレゼント買うの？）
☐ How will you spend this Christmas?（今年のクリスマスはどう過ごす？）

13 日本地理，どのくらい知っている？
Geography of Japan

　生徒は日本のことをどのくらい知っているでしょうか。比較級，最上級の学習を兼ね，トリビアクイズを作成し，それを Small Talk で，出し合わせてみましょう。

文法事項	比較（比較級・最上級）
主な表現	How much do you know about Japan? What is the highest mountain in Japan?　How high is Mt. Fuji? What is the second highest mountain in Japan? Mt. Asama is much lower than Kita-dake.　Where is Kita-dake? What is the largest prefecture in Japan? What is the oldest temple?　Who built it?　等
実施時期	中学2年　1月
留意点	「1番〜だ」は，the 〜est を用いて言い表しますが，「2番目に〜だ」は，the second 〜est と，序数を使って表します。教科書では，「1番〜だ」は扱いますが，「2番目に〜だ」は，あまり扱いません。決して難しくない表現ですので，活用できる表現となるように指導したいです。
応用・発展	World Geography ☞ Name the biggest country.〔1番大きい国はどこ？〕 Animals ☞ What animal can run the fastest?〔1番速く走る動物は？〕

Teacher's Talk

T : Hello. You live in Japan. Do you know about Japan very much? We, Japanese should know our country. O.K. Let's answer my quizzes. What is the longest river in Japan?（Ss: The Shinano River.）Yes. The longest river is the Shinano River. Then, how long is the river?　　S1: I don't know.

T : Please guess.　　S2: 1,000 km?

T : No, it is shorter than 1,000 km.　　S2: 500 km?

T : No, it is shorter than 500 km.　　S3: 300 km?

T : No, it is longer than 300 km.　　S4: 350 km?

T : Oh, it's close! It is 367 km long.

　　Today, we're going to talk about Japan.

中学**2**年 すらすら英会話

Let's talk about 'Geography of Japan.'

Today's Point 相手の発言を繰り返したり，相づちを打ったり，反応しましょう。

① How much do you know about Japan?

❶ I know about Japan. Please ask me.

② What is the highest mountain in Japan?

❷ It's easy. It's Mt. Fuji.

③ Correct! How high is Mt. Fuji?

❸ It's 3,775 meters high.

④ Close. It's 3,776 meters high. What is the second highest mountain?

❹ Umm .... Sorry, I have no idea. Give me some hints.

⑤ It's in Chubu area.

❺ I got it! Mt. Asama.

⑥ No. The answer is Kita-dake.

❻ I didn't know that.

⑦ Mt. Asama is lower than Kita-dake. Where is Kita-dake?

❼ I'm not sure, but in Yamanashi?

⑧ Your guess is right!

❽ Am I clever?

⑨ What is the largest prefecture in Japan?

❾ I know! It's Hokkaido.

⑩ Great! Then, what is the second largest prefecture?

❿ I think it's Iwate.

⑪ True! What is the oldest temple?

⓫ It's Asuka Temple.

⑫ Great! Who built it?

⓬ Sogano Umako built it.

Useful Expressions クイズで使える英語表現を使ってみましょう。

☐ Please ask me.（質問して）　☐ It's easy.（簡単）　　☐ Correct! / True!（正解！）

☐ I have no idea.（わからない）　☐ I got it!（わかった！）　☐ I didn't know that.（知らなかった）

☐ I'm not sure, but ....（よくわからないけど…）☐ That's true.（正しいです）☐ Close!（おしい！）

81

14 どの教科が好き？
School Subjects

「教科」は，生徒に共通する話題であり，比較を用いて様々なやり取りができます。１つの話題から，様々な質問をしたり，話題を広げたりしながら，会話の継続を図りましょう。

文法事項	比較（長い単語の比較級・最上級）　過去形（be 動詞・一般動詞）
主な表現	What subjects do you like?　Why do you like them?
	What do you want to be in the future?
	When did you begin to think that you want to be a tour guide?
	How about history?　What do you like about history?
	Who teaches history?　How do you like his class?
	Which is more interesting, English or history?
	What subjects don't you like?　等
実施時期	中学２年　２月
留意点	中学生ともなると，教科そのものが面白いという内発的な動機により学習することもありますが，一方，将来の自己実現のために学習するという自己決定理論でいう統合的調整の目的が生まれます。なぜ勉強をするのかを考えさせるためにも，教科について Small Talk させ，勉強の意味に気付かせていきましょう。
応用・発展	Favorite Food
	☞ What food do you like the best?〔食べ物は何が１番好き？〕
	Sport ☞ What is the most exciting sport?〔１番ワクワクするスポーツは？〕

Teacher's Talk

T: You study many subjects at school. What are they?

Ss: English, Japanese ....（T: 教科名を表すイラストを黒板に貼る）

T: What subjects do you like?　　　　　　　　　　Ss: I like P.E. ...

T: What is the most interesting subject?　　　　　S1: Math.

T: Math is the most interesting.

　　What is the second most interesting subject?　S1: Science.

T: Which do you like better, P.E. or home economics?　S1: I like P.E.

T: What subject are you good at?　　　　　　　　S2: I'm good at math.

T: So, you like studying math, right?　　　　　　S2: Yes, I do.

82

Let's talk about 'School Subjects.'

Today's Point 1つの話題から，色々な話題へ広げる力を付けましょう。

① What subjects do you like?

❶ I like English and history.

② Why do you like them?

❷ Because they are fun and interesting.

③ What do you want to be in the future?

❸ I want to be a tour guide.

④ Why do you want to be a tour guide?

❹ I like to travel and talk with people.

⑤ When did you decide to be a tour guide?

❺ When I was a fifth grader, I learned English. The class was fun. I started to like English.

⑥ How about history? What do you like about history?

❻ To know Japanese history is fun. My favorite era is Sengoku. I am a fan of Toyotomi Hideyoshi.

⑦ Who teaches history?

❼ Mr. Sato does.

⑧ How do you like his class?

❽ It's very interesting.

⑨ Which is more interesting, English or history?

❾ Both are interesting, but English is more interesting than history.

⑩ What subjects don't you like?

❿ I do not like math or science.

Useful Expressions

☐ How about history?（歴史はどう？）
☐ I am a fan of ～.（～のファンです）
☐ How do you like his class?（彼の授業はどう？）
☐ Both are interesting.（両方とも面白いです）
☐ I do not like math or science.（数学と理科が好きではないです）

15 私の好きなこと
My Favorite Things

　生徒は何をすることが好きなのでしょうか。「好きなこと」については，比較的，話しやすい話題と言えます。映画，歌，食べ物，本，漫画，スポーツなどなど，様々かと思います。

文法事項	受け身　不定詞（名詞的用法）

主な表現	What do you like to do in your free time?　For example? They look delicious.　Is it easy to make cookies? How long does it take you to make them? Is that sung by MISIA?　Do you like to read books?　等

実施時期	中学2年　3月

留意点	2年生のこの時期は，受け身を学習しますので，それを使って Small Talk をさせたいのですが，受け身が使える場面が，都合よく出てくるとは限りません。 元々，「思考力，判断力，表現力等」の活動は，既習表現の中から適切な表現を選択することに意味があります。無理に使わせようとすることなく Small Talk をさせましょう。

応用・発展	Local Food 　　☞ What is a famous local food in our town?〔有名な特産物は？〕 Movies ☞ What movies are loved by your friends?〔人気のある映画は？〕

Teacher's Talk

T : What do you like to do in your free time? As you know, I like travelling.
This picture was taken in Tokushima. I enjoyed the festival, Awa-Odori. It is held from August 12th to 15th every year. The dance is loved by many people. I am not good at dancing, but I enjoyed it. I went to the Kotohiki Park. A big coin can be seen there. This is the picture. It is a sand picture. It is made from sand. What do you like to do in your free time?　S1: I like to sing songs.

T : What songs do you like?　　　　　　　S1: I like Sekai-no-owari's songs.

T : What is your favorite song?　　　　　　S1: "Yokohama Blues."

T : When was it released?　　　　　　　　S1: In 2019.

T : Are you a good singer?　　　　　　　　S1: Yes, I'm good at singing.

T : Wow, I want to listen to your songs!　　S1: Some day.

Let's talk about 'My Favorite Things.'

Today's Point 質問に答えたら数文付け足して，詳しく説明しましょう。

① What do you like to do in your free time?

❶ I have many favorite things to do.

② For example?

❷ I like making cookies.
These cookies are made by me.

③ They look delicious.
Is it easy to make cookies?

❸ Yes. My family loves my cookies.
I make cookies on weekend.

④ How long does it take you to make them?

❹ It takes me for one hour and a half.

⑤ What else do you like?

❺ I like to listen to music.

⑥ What is your favorite song?

❻ I like "Ai-no-katachi."

⑦ Is that sung by MISIA?

❼ Yes, it is sung by MISIA.
It was the theme tune of the TV drama "Gibo-to-musume-no-burusu."

⑧ Do you like to read books?

❽ Yes. Look at this.
This book was written by Higashino Keigo. It is a detective story.

⑨ Do you see movies?

❾ Yes, I like watching anime.
This anime was released last year.

Useful Expressions

☐ What do you like to do in your free time?（暇な時に何するのが好き？）
☐ How long does it take you to make them?（作るのにどのくらい時間がかかる？）
☐ It takes me for one hour and a half.（1時間半かかります）

85

hi to ku chi ei go

ひとくち英語 ②

31 ⇒ 60

㉛ そうだね。／知っています。
㉜ 知らない。
㉝ 知っていましたか？
㉞ 知らなかった。
㉟ 完璧！
㊱ そう思いませんか？
㊲ 私もそう思います。
㊳ ちょっと待ってもらえますか？
㊴ あなたの言うことはわかります。
㊵ こんな風に考えてみたら？
㊶ どのくらい大きいの？
㊷ このくらい。
㊸ いくらかかったの？
㊹ 何か例を話して。
㊺ もちろん。
㊻ 簡単です。
㊼ 本気ですか？
㊽ 本気です。
㊾ 冗談でしょ？
㊿ 私は真剣です。
(51) 残念です。
(52) 面白いね。
(53) おめでとう。
(54) 信じて！
(55) よかったね。
(56) なるほど…。
(57) 質問していい？
(58) いい質問だね。
(59) ちょっと考えさせて。
(60) 何が起こったの？

㉛ I know.
㉜ I don't know. / I have no idea.
㉝ Did you know that?
㉞ I didn't know that.
㉟ Perfect!
㊱ Don't you think so?
㊲ I think so too.
㊳ Just a minute, please.
㊴ I see your point.
㊵ Think of it like this.
㊶ How big?
㊷ This size.
㊸ How much did it cost?
㊹ Give me some examples.
㊺ Of course. / Sure.
㊻ It's easy. / It's a piece of cake.
㊼ Are you sure?
㊽ I mean it.
㊾ You're kidding.
㊿ I'm serious. / I'm not kidding.
(51) I'm sorry. / That's too bad.
(52) That's interesting.
(53) Congratulations.
(54) Trust me!
(55) Good for you. / Lucky you.
(56) That makes sense. / I see.
(57) Can I ask you a question?
(58) Good question.
(59) Let me think.
(60) What happened (to you)?

中学3年で扱いたい！
トピック別
「すらすら英会話」
15

1 お互いを知ろう②
Get to know each other

　2年生で学習した表現を復習しながら，相手を知ることを目的としたSmall Talkをします。生徒がどのくらい会話が続けられるか観察してみましょう。そこから指導が始まります。

文法事項	復習（未来形・不定詞・動名詞・比較・助動詞・There is/are 構文）
主な表現	Are you interested in music?　What song by Seka-owa do you like? What do you like to do at home?　Is it fun for you to watch YouTube? Are there any interesting YouTube channels? What is the most interesting YouTube channel? Do you have anything to do tonight?　What will you do tonight? I must finish reading it and return. Which do you like better, "ハイキュー!!" or "One Piece?"　等
実施時期	中学3年　4月中旬
留意点	英語では，人と出会った時，必ずと言っていいほど相手の様子を尋ねる挨拶をします。How are you? 以外にも，What's up? / How's everything? / How's life? / How's it going? / How are you doing? など，様々あります。返答の仕方も様々ありますので，表現を教えていくとよいでしょう。
応用・発展	Favorite Things to Do 　☞ Are there any favorite things to do? 〔何か好きなことは？〕 Plans for Tonight ☞ What will you do tonight? 〔今夜の予定は？〕

Teacher's Talk

T: Hi. Welcome to my English class. I hope you study English hard and enjoy talking in English this year. Do you like English?　S1: Umm ..., yes.

T: What subject do you like the best?　S2: I like science.

T: Why do you like it?　S2: It's fun.

T: How about English class?　S2: I don't like it very much.

T: I hope you enjoy my class.
　 What do you like to do in your free time?　S3: I like playing baseball.

T: Yes, you are a good baseball player.

Get to know each other.

Today's Point たくさん質問して，友だちのことをよく知りましょう。

① Hi, there! How's it going?
❶ Pretty good. How about you?

② Good. Are you interested in music?
❷ Yes, I am. I like Sekai-no-owari.

③ What song by Seka-owa do you like?
❸ I like the song "RAIN." It's a theme tune of "メアリと魔女の花."

④ Yes! I know the song. What do you like to do at home?
❹ I like watching YouTube.

⑤ Is it fun for you to watch YouTube?
❺ Yes, it is.

⑥ Are there any interesting YouTube channels?
❻ Yes, there are many interesting channels.

⑦ What is the most interesting YouTube channel?
❼ I think Yonino-Channel is the most interesting.

⑧ Do you have anything to do tonight?
❽ Yes, I do.

⑨ What will you do tonight?
❾ I'm going to read "ハイキュー!!." I must finish reading it and return.

⑩ Which do you like better, "ハイキュー!!" or "One Piece?"
❿ I like "One Piece" better.

Useful Expressions 色々なあいさつの返答を使い分けてみましょう。

☐ Going well!（順調！） ☐ Same as usual.（いつも通りかな） ☐ Not too good.（イマイチ）
☐ Awful!（最悪！） ☐ Pretty good!（結構いいよ！） ☐ Excellent! / Terrific!（最高！）
☐ I'm good. / Not bad. / I'm OK.（まあまあ） ☐ Couldn't be better!（最高です！）

89

2 星座は何座？
The Zodiac Sign

　Small Talk で「星座」を話題にします。1日の運試しに，テレビで星占いを見てくる生徒もいることでしょう。自分の星座くらいは言えるようにしたいものです。英語版の占いを配って読ませるのも，読みのよい練習になりますね。

文法事項	過去形（be 動詞・一般動詞）　未来形（will）　比較（比較級・最上級）
主な表現	When is your birthday?　What's your sign?　When were you born? Where were you born?　What do you want for your birthday? Do you believe in horoscopes?　Do you check your horoscopes? What is your horoscope today?　What is the luckiest sign today? Will it come true?　等
実施時期	中学3年　4月下旬
留意点	星座によっては，気を付けなくてはいけない発音があります。例えば，Gemini は「ジェミナイ」と読み，Pisces は「パイシース」という発音になります。また，「私は山羊座です」と言う時は，冠詞の a/an が付いて，I am a Capricorn. または，My sign is a Capricorn. と言います。
応用・発展	*Omikuji* 　☞ Do you like to draw a fortune slip at temple?〔おみくじは好き？〕 Blood Type 　☞ What is your blood type?〔血液型は何型？〕

Teacher's Talk

T : Good morning, what do you do in the morning? I always check my horoscope on TV. This is today's horoscope. My birthday is January 19th, so my sign is a Capricorn. I am not good today. My sign is the 9th luckiest. What is your sign?

　(Ss: ...) When is your birthday?　　　　　S1: My birthday is May 3rd.

T : Wow, your birthday is coming soon.

　What do you want this year?　　　　　　S1: I want a new racket.

T : Good! When is your birthday?　　　　　S2: My birthday is August 1st.

　So, your sign is a Leo. Today's horoscope says when you study, it is good to cooperate with your friends.　　　　　S2: Really? I'll do that.

Let's talk about 'The Zodiac Sign.'

Today's Point 自分の思いや考えを自由自在に英語で伝えてみましょう。

① When is your birthday?
❶ My birthday is January 19th.

② What's your sign?
❷ My sign is a Capricorn.

③ When were you born?
❸ I was born in 2009.

④ Where were you born?
❹ I was born in Tokyo.
I was born and raised in Tokyo.

⑤ What do you want for your birthday?
❺ I want nothing special.
I want to eat delicious steak!

⑥ Do you believe in horoscopes?
❻ If it is good for me, I believe. If it is not good, I don't care about it.

⑦ Do you check your horoscope?
❼ Yes. I enjoy daily horoscopes on TV.

⑧ What is your horoscope today?
❽ My sign is the 3rd luckiest.
I should be quiet and listen to the others. My lucky color is purple.

⑨ Will it come true?
❾ I believe so.

⑩ What is the luckiest sign today?
❿ It's a Leo.

Useful Expressions 英語の星座名を覚えましょう。

☐ 牡羊座 (Aries)　　☐ 牡牛座 (Taurus)　　☐ 双子座 (Gemini)　　☐ かに座 (Cancer)
☐ 獅子座 (Leo)　　☐ 乙女座 (Virgo)　　☐ 天秤座 (Libra)　　☐ さそり座 (Scorpio)
☐ 射手座 (Sagittarius)　　☐ 山羊座 (Capricorn)　　☐ 水瓶座 (Aquarius)　　☐ うお座 (Pisces)

3 修学旅行はどこに行くの？
School Trip

　3年生にとって，修学旅行は楽しみな行事の1つと言えます。修学旅行でどこに行くのか，楽しみにしていることなど話題にして，Small Talk を行いましょう。

文法事項	現在完了形（完了・経験）　不定詞（疑問詞＋不定詞）
	未来形（be going to / will）
主な表現	Are you looking forward to going on a school trip?
	Where are you going?　Have you decieded on the plan yet?
	Have you ever been to Kyoto or Nara?
	Where do you want to go in Kyoto?　How will you go there?　等
実施時期	中学3年　5月中旬
留意点	技能は繰り返す中で身に付いていきます。答えたら，複数文，付け足しながら，自分の思いや考えを詳しく説明させたいです。Are you looking forward to going on a school trip? に対して，Of course, I am. と答えた後，I'm looking forward to it very much. と very much を付け足すだけでも，相手意識を持った対話となります。
応用・発展	Golden Week ☞ Do you have any plans for Golden Week?〔GW の予定は？〕
	School Trip at Elementary School　☞ Where did you go?〔どこに行った？〕

Teacher's Talk

T : You are going on a school trip next month. Are you looking forward to it?
　　When I was a junior high school student, I went to Kyoto and Nara on a school trip. I had a good time there. I remember Kiyomizu-dera Temple. It was one of the most fun places to visit for me. There were three waterfalls. One was for long life, the second one was for love, and the third one was for good luck for studying. We must not drink all of them. Which one do you drink? I drank the third one. I saw many foreign people. I talked to them because I like English and I wanted to try my English. By the way, have you decided where to go?

S1: Yes.

T : What's your plan? Where are you going on the first day?　　S1: Nara.

T : Where are you going in Nara?　　　　　　　　　　　　　S1: Todai-ji.

92

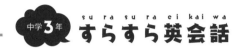

Let's talk about 'School Trip.'

Today's Point 相手に尋ねられたら，いくつかの情報を足し，詳しく伝えるようにしましょう。

① Are you looking forward to going on a school trip?
❶ Of course, I am.
　I'm looking forward to it very much.

② Where are you going?
❷ We're going to Kyoto and Nara.

③ Which are you looking forward to, visiting Kyoto or visiting Nara?
❸ I prefer Nara to Kyoto.
　I want to see old temples in Nara.

④ Have you decided on the plan yet?
❹ No, we haven't.
　Our group is discussing where to go.

⑤ Have you ever been to Kyoto or Nara?
❺ No, I haven't.
　It is my first time visiting there.

⑥ Where do you want to go in Kyoto?
❻ I want to go to Arashiyama.

⑦ What do you want to do there?
❼ I want to walk through the bamboo forest. I want to eat sweets too.

⑧ How will you go there?
❽ We haven't decided how to go there, but maybe we'll take a train and get off at the Arashiyama Station.

⑨ When are you going on a school trip?
❾ We're going on a school trip on June 22nd.

Useful Expressions

☐ I'm looking forward to 〜. (〜を楽しみにしている)　☐ I prefer A to B. (BよりAを好む)

☐ Have you planned yet? (もう計画をたてましたか？)

☐ Have you ever been to 〜? (〜に行ったことがありますか？)

☐ We are discussing where to go. (どこに行こうか話し合っています)

93

4 どんな料理を作る？
Cooking

　生徒は家で料理をするのでしょうか。どんな料理を作るのでしょうか。みなさんの得意料理は何でしょうか。食育を絡め，生徒と料理の話題で Small Talk をしてみましょう。

文法事項	不定詞（副詞的用法）　接続詞（if, when）
主な表現	Do you cook?　What do you cook?　What is your best dish? I have no time to cook on weekdays.　Is it easy for you to cook? It takes time.　How long does it take to cook croquette? How do you cook croquette?　等
実施時期	中学3年　6月
留意点	料理を話題にしつつ，どのように作るのかが説明できるように，語彙を導入したり，簡単な表現は覚えさせるとよいでしょう。①皮をむく（peel）②ゆでる（boil）③炒める（stir-fry）④混ぜる（mix）⑤〜を鍋に入れる（put 〜 in the pot）⑥魚を焼く（grill）⑦切る（cut/mince）　等
応用・発展	Favorite Dish ☞ What's your favorite dish?〔好きな料理は？〕 Desserts ☞ What kind of desserts do you like?〔好きなデザートは？〕

Teacher's Talk

T: This is my dinner last night.（写真）I cook every day. My best dishes are hamburger steak, fried rice, and croquette. My daughters love to eat them. Every year, I'm thinking that I want to learn more new dishes. Last year, I learned how to cook 生姜焼き, gratin, and シュウマイ. シューマイ is very delicious. This year, I want to learn how to cook 八宝菜, きんぴらごぼう, and I want to try roast beef. Do you cook?（Ss: Yes. / No.）

T: What do you cook?	S1: I cook curry.
T: Good! Do you like cooking?	S1: Yes, I do.
T: When do you cook? Do you cook every day?	S1: No. Only on weekend.
T: Do you make cookies?	S1: No.
T: Do you cook, S2?	S2: Yes.
T: What do you cook?	S2: I make *ramen*.

Let's talk about 'Cooking.'

Today's Point 質問するだけでなく，自分のことも伝えてから質問しましょう。

① I like cooking. Do you like cooking?

❶ Yes, I do. I love cooking.

② Good. I like to cook *oyako-don*.
What do you cook?

❷ I cook fried rice, curry and rice, *miso* soup and others.

③ What is the best dish to cook?

❸ The best dishes to cook are hamburger steak and croquette.
They are loved by my family.

④ Do you cook every day?

❹ No, I don't. I cook on weekend.
I have no time to cook on weekdays.

⑤ Is it easy for you to cook?

❺ No. It's not easy, but it's fun.

⑥ Is it difficult to cook croquette?

❻ Yes, it is. It's difficult and takes time.

⑦ How long does it take to cook it?

❼ It takes about 1 hour and a half.

⑧ How do you cook croquette?

❽ First, I peel potatoes, and boil them.
Second, I smash the potatoes. Third, I stir-fry ground meat and onion.
Fourth, I mix the mashed potato with ground meat and onion.

⑨ When can you cook me a croquette?

❾ No kidding!

Useful Expressions

☐ What is the best you cook dish?（得意料理は何？）
☐ I have no time to ～.（～する時間がない）　☐ It takes time.（時間がかかる）
☐ How long does it take to ～?（～するのにどのくらい時間がかかるの？）
☐ Is it easy for you to ～?（～はあなたにとって簡単？）

5 修学旅行はどうだった？
How was your school trip?

修学旅行前にも Small Talk をしましたので，修学旅行後にも，Small Talk を行い，どんな修学旅行であったのか，伝え合わせましょう。

文法事項	過去形（be 動詞・一般動詞） 接続詞（if, when）
主な表現	How was your school trip? What was the most impressive thing about your school trip? What did you like about Horyu-ji Temple? Did you sleep well? Did you buy any souvenirs? Who did you buy for? On the second day, where did you go? If you visit Kyoto again, where do you want to go? 等
実施時期	中学3年 6月下旬
留意点	修学旅行が終わると，おそらく授業で，その体験を英語で伝えることを行うかと思います。修学旅行について伝え合う学習をした後，帯学習の Small Talk で修学旅行を扱い，伝えることに習熟させます。また，Let me know about your school trip? という即興的に発表させることも取り入れたいです。
応用・発展	Last Weekend ⤳ How was your last weekend?〔先週末はどうだった？〕 Music Festival ⤳ How was the Music Festival?〔音楽祭はどうだった？〕

Teacher's Talk

T : The most fun school event is over. How was your school trip?
　Was it fun?（Ss: Yes.）

T : What is the most impressive thing about your school trip?

S1: I remember Kinkaku-ji. It was gold and shiny.

T : Yes, your most impressive thing is Kinkaku-ji. How about you, S2?

S2: I liked Todai-ji Temple. Daibutsu was big. Many deer came to me.

T : Did you take a picture with the deer?

S2: Yes. I gave them 'Shika Sembei.'

T : Right. Were you afraid of deer?

S2: Yes. They were around me and wanted to eat *sembei*. I was really afraid.

How was your school trip?

Today's Point アイコンタクトやジェスチャーを忘れずに Small Talk をしましょう。

① How was your school trip?

❶ It was wonderful.

② What was the most impressive thing about your school trip?

❷ I remember Horyu-ji Temple.

③ What did you like about Horyu-ji Temple?

❸ I have seen a picture of Horyu-ji Temple in a history book, but I haven't seen it with my own eyes. So, when I saw it, I was so impressed.

④ Did you sleep well?

❹ Yes, I enjoyed talking too.

⑤ Did you buy any souvenirs?

❺ Yes, I did.

⑥ Who did you buy for?

❻ I bought souvenirs for my family.

⑦ Did they like them?

❼ Yes, they liked my souvenirs.

⑧ On the second day, where did you go?

❽ My group went to Nanzen-ji Temple.

⑨ Did you eat *yu-dofu*?

❾ Of course. Nanzen-ji Temple is famous for *yu-dofu*. It was delicious.

⑩ If you visit Kyoto again, where do you want to go?

❿ I want to visit Arashiyama. My friend said that it was good.

Useful Expressions

☐ How was your school trip?（修学旅行はどうだった？）
☐ What was the most impressive thing?（一番印象に残っていることは？）
☐ Nanzen-ji Temple is famous for *yu-dofu*.（南禅寺は，湯豆腐で有名です）

6 都会がいい？　田舎がいい？
City or Countryside

　意見文を Small Talk で扱います。最もポピュラーな「都会がいいか，田舎がいいか」で，ディスカッションさせます。

文法事項	不定詞（副詞的用法）　構文（主語＋ be 動詞＋形容詞＋ that ...）
主な表現	Which would you prefer to live in, a city or the countryside? Can you tell me why?　What else do you like to live in the countryside? But is it inconvenient to go shopping, right? What do you like to do in cities?　I can see your point. That makes sense.　I'm glad that you know my idea.　等
実施時期	中学3年　7月
留意点	意見を言う時は，英語の三段論法を用います。まず，最初に結論（Topic Sentence）を言います。次にその理由（Supporting Sentences）を言います。最後に，再度，結論（Concluding Sentence）を言います。この型を意識させると，まとまりのある話ができるようになります。
応用・発展	Disneyland or Universal Studio ⤵ Which do you like?〔どっちが好き？〕 Summer or Winter 　⤵ Which do you like better, summer or winter?〔夏か冬か？〕

Teacher's Talk

T : I was born and raised in Higashiyamato city, Tokyo. I am from Tokyo. My city is rich in nature. Look.（写真）This is Tama Lake. You can see a beautiful lake. You can enjoy cherry blossoms in spring. I used to run along the lake when I was a junior high school student. I like nature, so I wanted to live in the countryside. Look.（写真）This is a picture of Chichibu, Saitama. I became a teacher in Chichibu. There is a lot of nature in my city. You can see rivers, mountains, beautiful stars. I love the countryside.

T : What do you think?	S1: I like a city.
T : You like living in a city?	S1: Yes.
T : Why do you like living in a city?	S1: I can buy many things.
T : What do you think, S2?	S2: I like living in a city too.

Let's talk about 'City' or 'Countryside.'

Today's Point 内容を整理して、伝えたいことの順番を考え話しましょう。

① Which would you prefer to live in, a city or the countryside?

❶ I would prefer to live in the countryside.

② Can you tell me why?

❷ Sure. I like to live in peace.
I do not like noisy places.
Cities are too busy.
I want to live in a quiet place.

③ What else do you like to live in the countryside?

❸ I can see beautiful stars.
I can grow vegetables.
I can play outside.
The air is clean.
Water is fresh and delicious.

④ But is it inconvenient to go shopping, right?

❹ No, if you have a car, you can drive to the nearest shopping mall.

⑤ I like living in a city.
In a city, we have everything.

❺ What do you like to do in cities?

⑥ I can go to a theater and enjoy seeing movies, going shopping, having a delicious food.

❻ I can see your point.
For me, I live in the countryside and go to cities to shop.
Don't you think so?

⑦ That makes sense.

❼ I'm glad that you know my ideas.

Useful Expressions 意見について反応する表現を使ってみましょう。

☐ I agree/disagree with your idea.（あなたの意見に賛成／反対です）
☐ What do you think?（あなたはどう思いますか？） ☐ I think so too.（私もそう思います）
☐ I see your point.（あなたの言うことはわかります） ☐ That makes sense.（わかります）

7 次の目標は？
What's your next goal?

　生徒の多くは，夏をもって部活動を終えます。部活動は生徒にとって，１つの大きな思い出になっていることと思います。そして部活動を終えたら，いよいよ進路に向け，高校入試の勉強等が始まります。この時期，うまく次の目標に向かえるかが生徒にとってはとても大事になってきます。これからのことについて語り合わせましょう。

文法事項	過去形 (be 動詞・一般動詞)　未来形 (be going to / will)
主な表現	How was your summer vacation? What did you do in your summer vacation? What's your next goal?　What are you doing for that? Hang in there!　等
実施時期	中学３年　９月
留意点	今回の Small Talk は，２つの表現が入っています。１つは，夏におこなったこと，もう１つは，これからの目標を伝え合うということです。明示的に，黒板に２つのことを伝え合うように示しておくとよいでしょう。
応用・発展	Things to Do ☞ What will you do tonight? 〔やらなくてはいけないこと〕 Achieving Goals 　☞ What is important to achieve your goal? 〔ゴール達成に向けて〕

Teacher's Talk

T : How was your summer vacation? We had a tennis tournament this summer. The pair of Takeru and Hiroshi won first place, and they went to the prefectural tournament. They won the first match but lost the second one. They played very good. Now, a new team has just start practicing for the autumn tournament.

T : How did your team go?　　　　　　S1: Our team got second place.

T : Great! Which school won first place?　S1: Nishi JHS did.

T : Now, you quit your team.

　　What is the next goal for you?　　　S1: To study.

100

中学3年 すらすら英会話
su ra su ra ei kai wa

What's your next goal?

Today's Point 相手の言いたいことを推測して，言ってあげましょう。

① How was your summer vacation?

❶ It was good.

② What did you do in your summer vacation?

❷ I had a judo ....

③ <u>Tournament?</u>

❸ Yes, judo tournament. Our team won the local tournament, and we joined the prefectural one.

④ What was the result of the prefectural tournament?

❹ We won the first two matches, but we lost the third one. We were in the top 16. It became a good memory for me. Now, I ... 引退 ... .

⑤ <u>You quit the judo team?</u>

❺ Yes, I quit the judo team.

⑥ What's your next goal?

❻ My next goal is to study hard for the examination.

⑦ What are you doing for that?

❼ I've been trying to study for three hours every day at home.

⑧ Great. I hope your dream will come true.

❽ Thanks.

⑨ Hang in there!

❾ Yes, I will.

Useful Expressions

☐ I quit the judo team last month. （先月で，柔道部を引退しました）

☐ What was the result of the prefectural tournament? （県大会の結果は？）

☐ What is your next goal? （次の目標は？）

101

8 どんな本を読んでいる？
Reading a Book

　学校によっては，朝読書の時間を設けている所があるかと思います。生徒は，どんな本を読んでいて，どんな本が好きなのでしょうか。読書をテーマに Small Talk をします。

文法事項	現在進行形　受け身　関係代名詞 (主格)　後置修飾 (過去分詞)
主な表現	Are you reading a book?　What are you reading? I'm reading a book written by Kozuki Hinowa. That sounds interesting.　What is the story about? It is a story about a boy who lives in an apartment and grows up. Who is the main character?　How do you like the book?　等
実施時期	中学3年　10月上旬
留意点	「今，何読んでいるの？」は，What book are you reading now? と言います。 通常，現在進行形は，「今現在，やっていること」を言いますが，日本語と同様，「今現在，継続して進行していること」にも使います。例えば，「韓国語を勉強しているの？」は，Are you studying Korean? ですし，「柔道はまだやっているの？」は，Are you still practicing judo? となります。
応用・発展	Movies ☞ Are there any movies that you like?〔何か好きな映画はある？〕 Songs ☞ What music are you listening to?〔どんな音楽を聴いているの？〕

Teacher's Talk

T : What are you reading? I like reading books. I like to read books written by Uchida Yasuo. His books are so interesting. They are detective stories. I like detective stories. When I have free time, I read a book.

T : What are you reading now?　　　　S1 : I am reading a book, "Battery."
　　Yes, I know!
　　It is written by Asano Atsuko.　　S1 : Yes, written by Asano Atsuko.

T : What's the story about?　　　　　S1 : It is a story about baseball players.

T : How do you like the book?　　　　S1 : It's fun. I'm looking forward to the end.

T : Nice. How many volumes are there?　S1 : Six volumes. I'm reading volume 3.

T : So you have three more to read.　　S1 : Yes.

Let's talk about 'Reading a Book.'

Today's Point 1つの話題を深めたり，広げたりして対話を続けましょう。

① Are you reading a book? ① Yes, I am.

② What are you reading? ② I'm reading a book written by Kozuki Hinowa.

③ What is the title of the book? ③ It is "妖怪アパートの幽雅な日常."

④ That sounds interesting. What is the story about? ④ It is a story about a boy who lives in an apartment and grows up.

⑤ Who is the main character? ⑤ The main character is Inaba Yushi.

⑥ How do you like the book? ⑥ It is interesting to read what will happen next.

⑦ How many volumes are there? ⑦ There are 10 volumes.

⑧ Wow, so many! How many volumes have you read? ⑧ I've just read the volume 4.

⑨ Do you read comic books? ⑨ Yes. I like "ハイキュー!!."

⑩ Who wrote the book? ⑩ It was written by Furudate Haruichi.

⑪ Do you have the comic books? ⑪ No. I borrow books from the library.

Useful Expressions

☐ What is the title of the book?（本のタイトルは？）
☐ That sounds interesting.（面白そうだね）　☐ What is the story about?（どんな内容なの？）　☐ Who is the main character?（主人公は誰？）
☐ How many volumes are there?（何巻あるの？）　☐ Who wrote the book?（作者は？）

9 あなたの夢は？
Dreams for the Future

　3年生は部活も終え，うまく次の目標を立てて，それに向けて取り組めている生徒はいいですが，目標を失ったり，計画が実行できていなかったりする生徒もいることでしょう。ここで，将来の夢について語り合い，もう一度，目標を確認する Small Talk としたいです。

文法事項	現在形（be 動詞・一般動詞）　動名詞
主な表現	What is your dream?　What are you doing to make the dream come true? So am I.　How is your study? What subject do you have to study harder? What do you do between your studies? How long have you been thinking to be a lawyer?　等
実施時期	中学3年　10月下旬
留意点	夢を生徒に語らせる時，やはり大事なことは，教師の夢を語ることです。教師が中学生の頃，どんな夢があり，それに向けてどんな努力をしてきたのかを素直に生徒に語ります。そして，今，何のために勉強しているのかを生徒に再確認させる時間としたいです。
応用・発展	Dairy Routine ☞ What do you do after school?〔放課後，何しているの？〕 What's up? ☞ What's up?〔最近どう？〕

Teacher's Talk

T : Hello, class. What do you do after school? I believe you are studying to make your dreams come true. When I was a junior high school student, I was thinking to become an English teacher. To be a teacher, I had to graduate from university. To enter a university, I needed to graduate from high school. So, I studied hard for the entrance examination after school. Between the studies, I sometimes went to school to play soccer and basketball. Also, I played the guitar when I was tired of studying.

T : What is your dream?　　　　　　　　　　　　S1: I want to be a programmer.

T : Good. How long have you been thinking to be a programmer?　S1: Since I was 10.

T : What are you doing to make your dream come true?　　　　　S1: I study.

中学3年 すらすら英会話

Let's talk about 'Dreams for the Future.'

Today's Point 話そうとすることを整理して，自分の考えを伝えましょう。

① What is your dream?

❶ My dream is to be a lawyer.

② Great! What are you doing to make the dream come true?

❷ I need to go to university to study about law. So, I must go to high school.
Now, I am studying hard to pass the entrance examination.

③ Right. So am I. How is your study going?

❸ My scores for the test aren't good enough.

④ What subject do you have to study harder?

❹ I must especially study math hard. Math is too difficult.

⑤ How about English?

❺ English is fine. I like English, and my scores are good.

⑥ Good. What do you do between your studies?

❻ When I am tired of studying, I often go outside and play basketball. It is a good refreshment for me.

⑦ How long have you been thinking to be a lawyer?

❼ When I was a 5th grader, I watched a TV drama about a lawyer.
I was interested in the job, and I started to think to help people by the law.

Useful Expressions

☐ I am studying for the entrance examination. — So am I. （私もです）

☐ What are you doing to make your dream come true? （夢実現のために何をしていますか？）

☐ How long have you been thinking to be a lawyer? （いつから弁護士になりたいと思っているの？）

10 あなたの好きな言葉は？
Favorite Word or Phrase

　言葉には力があります。言葉によって勇気づけられることは多々あります。みなさんが好きな言葉は何でしょうか。私の好きな言葉に，「終わりは始めなり」「後楽園」「住めば都」などがあります。みなさんの好きな言葉を生徒に伝え，Small Talk の話題としましょう。

文法事項	接続詞 (if, when)　関係代名詞 (目的格)

主な表現　Do you have some words or phrases that you like?

　　　　　Can you tell me one?　What does it mean?

　　　　　Can you give me some examples?

　　　　　Do you have some proverbs that you like?　等

実施時期　中学3年　11月

留意点　好きな言葉がすぐに出てくる生徒はいいですが，見つからない生徒もいることを考えると，Small Talk の前に，自分が話そうとすることを整理する時間をとりたいと思います。タブレットで名言やことわざを調べさせ，それについて伝え合わせます。

応用・発展　Motto ☞ What's your motto?〔あなたの座右の銘は？〕

　　　　　　Proverb ☞ What is your favorite proverb?〔好きなことわざは？〕

Teacher's Talk

T : Do you have any words or phrases that you like? If I am asked so, I will answer "Yes, I do." My favorite word is 'Dream.' Walt Disney, who created Disneyland, said "If you dream it, you can do it." This is a very famous phrase. So, if we do not dream, we cannot make our dreams come true. Every new year, I always write many dreams on my schedule book. This is it. (手帳を見せる) To make dreams is very fun. Well, ... Do you have any words or phrases that you like? What's your favorite word or phrase?

Let's surf in your tablet about famous words or phrases, 名言, or proverbs, ことわざ that you like.

Ss:（タブレットで調べる）

106

中学**3**年 su ra su ra ei kai wa **すらすら英会話**

Let's talk about 'Favorite Words or Phrases.'

Today's Point 複数の英文を用いて，自分の考えが伝わるように話しましょう。

① Do you have some words that you like?

❶ Yes. My favorite word is 'Love.' I want to be loved, and also I want to love people. I think we can save people if we have 'Love' for them.

② Do you have some phrases that you like?

❷ Yes, I do.

③ Can you tell me one?

❸ Sure. One of my favorite phrases is "The end is another start."

④ What does it mean?

❹ When we finish something, it means that we will start a new thing.

⑤ Can you give me some examples?

❺ I quit the soccer team this August. It is the end, but it is also another start. A new goal came to me that I study for the examination.

⑥ Do you have some proverbs that you like?

❻ Yes. When one door shuts, another opens. (捨てる神あれば，拾う神あり)

⑦ Why do you like it?

❼ My grandfather always says this. If something bad happens, we must not give up. Somebody will help us.

Useful Expressions

☐ Do you have some words or phrases that you like?（好きな言葉や表現はある？）

☐ Can you tell me one?（1つ教えてくれる？）　☐ What does it mean?（どういう意味？）

☐ Can you give me some examples?（何か例がありますか？）

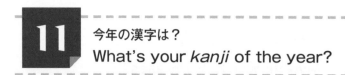

11 今年の漢字は？
What's your *kanji* of the year?

毎年，日本漢字能力検定協会が今年の漢字を発表しています。漢字を話題にしつつ，1年を振り返って，どんな1年であったのかを生徒にも漢字1字で表させたいです。

文法事項	構文 (it is ... for ... to ~)　関係代名詞（目的格・接触節）
主な表現	What is your *kanji* of the year?　Tell me why? What did you make?　Is it easy to make them? I want to eat macaron you make. Do you have any sweets that you want to make? Do you want to be a patissier? What do you want to be?　等
実施時期	中学3年　12月
留意点	教師が「今年の漢字」を生徒に話した後，この1年を生徒に振り返らせ，「今年の漢字」を考えさせます。考える時間を3分間とし，その時間で，今年の漢字を1字，選ばせます。それをタブレットで表示させ，Small Talk をさせるとよいでしょう。「今年の漢字」から，どんどん会話を膨らませていけるとよいです。
応用・発展	Memories of This Year 　↪ What good memories do you have this year?〔今年のよい思い出〕 *Kanji* of the New Year 　↪ What is your hope for this year?〔今年どんな年にする？〕

Teacher's Talk

T: Time flies. We have only three weeks left of this year. How did you spend this year? Last week, a *kanji* of the year was announced. Do you remember what the *kanji* was?（Ss: 何だったっけ？／わ～，忘れた）　It was this *kanji*.（写真）
For me, my *kanji* is "減." My blood pressure was getting high, so I needed to reduce my blood pressure. I began walking around my house, and gradually I could lower my blood pressure. So, this is my *kanji* of the year.

T: What's your *kanji* of the year?（Ss: ....）O.K. I'll give you three minutes to think about it. If you come up with the *kanji* of the year, you write the *kanji* on the tablet. Later, show it to your partner and have a chat.

中学**3**年 **すらすら英会話**
su ra su ra ei kai wa

What's your *kanji* of the year?

Today's Point 1つの話題を深め，できるだけ詳しく話してみましょう。

① *Kanji* of the year was announced. Do you remember what the *kanji* was?

❶ Maybe, it was "税", tax.

② Right. What is your *kanji* of the year?

❷ Well, I think it's "甘", sweet.

③ Sweet? Tell me why?

❸ I tried making sweets, and I learned how to cook many sweets.

④ Nice! What did you make?

❹ I made chocolate cake, cookies, and macarons.

⑤ Macarons? Great! Is it easy to make them?

❺ It takes time, but it is easy.

⑥ I want to eat macaron you make.

❻ No kidding.

⑦ Do you have any sweets that you want to make?

❼ Yes. I want to make tart.

⑧ Do you want to be a patissier?

❽ No. I just enjoy myself.

⑨ What do you want to be?

❾ I want to work at the city hall.

⑩ A restaurant in the city hall?

❿ No way! I want to be an officer.

Useful Expressions

☐ Tell me why?（なぜか教えて）

☐ It takes time, but it is easy.（時間はかかるけど，簡単です）

☐ No kidding.（冗談でしょ）

☐ No way!（そうじゃない＝あり得ない！）

109

12 今年の夢は？
Dreams for This Year

　卒業まであと3か月となりました。中学校を卒業すると多くは離れ離れになり，一緒にいられる時間も僅かです。中学校を卒業して，生徒が頑張りたいことは何でしょうか。そんな夢ややりたいことを伝える Small Talk をしましょう。

文法事項	現在完了（経験）　不定詞（名詞的用法・副詞的用法）
主な表現	Happy new year.　What's your dream for the new year? Where do you want to go to study English?　Have you been abroad? Where have you been to? What do you want to try new things?　等
実施時期	中学3年　1月中旬
留意点	「内容を整理して話す」ということは，とても大事な話すことの力をなります。今年やりたいこと，今年の夢は，おそらく1つではなく，いくつもあるかと思います。そんな時に，内容を整理して，いくつ夢があって，その夢の理由を語ると，ちょっとした即興的な発表になります。また，タブレットを使って，やりたいことを箇条書きで書き示し，それを見せながらやってもよいでしょう。
応用・発展	Family Dreams ☞ What's your ideal family?〔理想の家族は？〕 New Year's Resolution 　☞ What's your New Year's resolution?〔新年の抱負は？〕

Teacher's Talk

T : Happy new year. How was your winter vacation?
　　Did you go to temple or shrine on New Year's?
　　When and where did you go?　　　　S1: I went to Chichibu shrine on Jan. 2nd.
T : Did you pray?　　　　　　　　　　　　S1: Yes.
T : I prayed that my daughter would have a baby.
　　What did you pray?　　　　　　　　　S1: Pass the exam.
T : Right. You prayed for passing the entrance exam. S1: Yes.
T : What do you want to do this year?　　　S2: I want to learn *shogi*.
T : Great. Have you tried it before?　　　　S2: Yes, I have tried it once.
T : This year, I have many things that I want to do.

中学3年 すらすら英会話

Let's talk about 'Dreams for This Year.'

Today's Point 話す内容を整理して，上手に相手に伝えましょう。

① Happy new year.

❶ Happy new year.

② What's your dream for the new year?

❷ Good question.
I have several dreams.
First, I want to pass the entrance examination.
Second, I want to go abroad to study English.
Third, I want to try something new.

③ Nice dreams!
Where do you want to go to study English?

❸ I'm thinking to go to Canada.
I like "Anne of Green Gables",
so I want to visit and see where the novel was set.

④ Have you been abroad?

❹ Yes, I have.

⑤ Where have you been to?

❺ I don't remember very much because I was little, but I have been to Singapore.

⑥ What do you want to try new things?

❻ I want to learn karate.
Ei-ei-ei----. Ya!

⑦ What was your New Year's resolution last year?

❼ Well ..., I forgot!

Useful Expressions

☐ Good question. （いい質問ですね）

☐ I don't remember very much. （よく覚えていません）

☐ What's your dream for the new year? （新年の目標は何ですか？）

☐ Have you been abroad? （外国に行ったことはあるの？）　☐ I forgot! （忘れた！）

111

13 100万円あったらどうする？
If you had one million yen, ...

　仮定法過去の話題の代表的に「100万円あったらどうする？」があります。授業でも，この話題は扱っているかと思います。授業で行ったことをSmall Talkで継続して行うことで，話すことに習熟するのではないかと思います。

文法事項	比較（長い単語の比較級・最上級）　過去形（be動詞・一般動詞）
主な表現	If you had one million yen, what would you do? What would you buy?　How long have you been using your smartphone? It costs less than 100,000 yen to buy a smartphone. What else would you use for?　等
実施時期	中学3年　1月下旬
留意点	3年生になると，Small Talkを3分ほど継続できる力を付けたいと思います。そのためには，相手の話を聞きながら，①話題を深めたり，②話題を広げたりしていけるように，指導していきたいと思います。
応用・発展	Doraemon 　☞If Doraemon were your friend, ...〔もしドラえもんが友だちなら？〕 Wishes 　☞If you could make three wishes come true, ...〔3つ夢が叶うとしたら？〕

Teacher's Talk

T : Wow, money is important. If we have no money, we cannot live. If we have no money, we cannot buy anything. How much money do you have? I don't have much money. I have spent my money on buying a house, a car, and I have spent money on travelling. I like to travel. If you had 1,000,000 yen, what would you do?　　S1: I would buy a lot of comic books.

T : Wow, how many books can you buy with 1,000,000 yen?

S1: Maybe, 1000 books.

T : Wow, you like reading. How about you, S2?

S2: I would save money.

T : What do you want to use the money in the future?

S2: I want to travel around the world.

中学**3**年 **すらすら英会話**
su ra su ra ei kai wa

If you had one million yen, ...

Today's Point 1つの話題から色々な話題へ広げながら，会話を3分程度続けましょう。

① If you had one million yen, what would you do?

❶ Good question.
   I would spend half of it and save the other half.

② Good! What would you buy?

❷ I would buy a new smartphone.

③ How long have you been using your smartphone?

❸ I've been using my smartphone since I entered JHS.
   So I've been using it for almost three years.

④ It costs less than 100,000 yen to buy a smartphone.
   What else would you spend it on?

❹ I don't want so many things, but I would spend it on buying clother.
   I would eat delicious *sushi*.
   I would go to Disneyland.
   I would take my family to Okinawa.

⑤ By the way, you like music, right. Would you go to concerts?

❺ That's a good idea.
   I would buy concert tickets as many as possible.

⑥ I don't think you can save the half of the money.

❻ Right. I would spend all of 1,000,000 yen.

⑦ So you wouldn't save money.

❼ No, I wouldn't. Maybe.

Useful Expressions

☐ How long have you been using your smartphone?（スマートフォンはどのくらい使っているの？）

☐ It costs less than 100,000 yen to buy a smartphone.（スマートフォンは10万円しませんね）

☐ So you wouldn't save money. — No, I wouldn't.（はい。貯金しません）

113

14 英語と私
English and I

　生徒にとって英語は何なのでしょうか。英語の授業についてはどう思っているのでしょうか。AIが発達し，英語を学ぶ意義って何なのでしょうか。卒業前にSmall Talkで話題にしてみましょう。

| 文法事項 | 接続詞 (if, when)　不定詞 (名詞的用法・副詞的用法)　比較 (最上級) |

| 主な表現 | What do you think about English?　Do we need to study English? |

Why do you think so?　Don't you think so?

Exactly.　What do you think about English class?

Did you enjoy the class?　What is the most fun subject?

If you study another language, what do you want to study?

Do you want to go abroad to study English?　等

| 実施時期 | 中学3年　2月 |

| 留意点 | 私はよく3年生の3学期の期末テストに，English and I というテーマで自由英作文をさせていました。分量は優に100語は超えていたと思います。テストにつなげるためにも，Small Talk を終えたら，ミニ作文をさせていくとよいでしょう。 |

| 応用・発展 | Travel ☞ Which country do you want to visit in the future?〔行きたい国は？〕 |

English Class

　　☞ What did you learn through English?〔英語を通して何を学んだ？〕

Teacher's Talk

T : What do you think about English? Do you like English? (Ss: Yes. / No.)
When I was in the 9th grade, I became to like English. It became fun to learn English. Learning English is fun, and talking with people from other countries is fun too. I like travelling abroad, so it's convenient if I can use it.

T : What do you think about English?　　　　　S1: I like English.

T : What do you like about English?　　　　　S1: I like to talk in English.

T : Good. Is it easy for you to talk in English?　S1: No, but it's fun.

T : Thank you. How about S2? Do you like English?　S2: No, I don't.

T : Why not?　　　　　　　　　　　　　　　S2: I like math better.

114

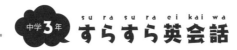

Let's talk about 'English and I.'

Today's Point 英語って必要なのでしょうか。みんなの考えを伝え合いましょう。

① What do you think about English?

① I think it's a useful subject.

② Do we need to study English?

② Yes, I think so.

③ Why do you think so?

③ If we can use English, we can communicate with people from foreign countries.

④ Right, but we have AI machines. If we use it, we don't have to learn English. Don't you think so?

④ I see your point. But I want to talk in person. Also, we can learn many cultures through studying English.

⑤ Exactly. What do you think about English class? Did you enjoy the class?

⑤ Yes, I enjoy the English class. It is fun for me to study English.

⑥ Is English the most fun subject?

⑥ Actually, no, it isn't.

⑦ What is the most fun subject?

⑦ Math is.

⑧ If you study another language, what do you want to study?

⑧ I want to study Korean. I like K-pop. I am a big fan of BTS.

⑨ Do you want to go abroad to study English?

⑨ Definitely.

Useful Expressions

☐ What do you think about English?（英語についてどう思う？）
☐ Don't you think so?（そう思いませんか？）　☐ I see your point.（あなたの言うことはわかります）
☐ I want to talk in person.（面と向かって話がしたいです）　☐ Exactly./Definitely.（確かに）

115

15 中学校の思い出は？
Memories of Junior High School

　小学校で生徒は，学校の思い出（My Best Memory）をテーマに，言語活動を行っています。中学校卒業を前に，中学校でも，生徒たちの思い出を共有させてみましょう。学校行事，部活，友だち，勉強，趣味など，生徒はどんなことに思い出があるのでしょうか。

文法事項	過去形（be 動詞・一般動詞）　比較（最上級）
主な表現	Do you have any memories of this school? What are good memories?　What was the best memory? Tell me about your school trip.　等
実施時期	中学3年　3月
留意点	生徒は日常生活を何気なく過ごし，あまり深く考えたことがないこともあるかと思います。今回のテーマ "Memories of Junior High School" も，改めて問われると，「何だろう？」と考えてしまうことかも知れません。そんな時には，考える時間を与え，内容を整理させる時間をとるとよいでしょう。
応用・発展	Memories of Your Life ☞ What are your good memories?〔よい思い出は？〕 Good bye, My Friends ☞ Talk with all the classmates!〔全員と英語で話そう！〕

Teacher's Talk

T : In three weeks, you are going to graduate from this school. Did you have good memories? What memories do you have? I hope you have made good memories. When I was a junior high school student, I was on the soccer team. My team was weak. Then we had a transfer student from other school where the soccer team was strong. The student was on the soccer team. Soon he became a regular member of our team. Just before graduating from school, we had a sports festival at school. I joined the soccer game. I played against his team. I ran and ran and tried to get a score very hard. But my team lost it. I was lying on the ground. Then the transfer student came up to me and showed his hand. He took my hand, and he made me stand up. We didn't talk a lot with him. It was just a moment, but I still remember that.

What are your good memories?

中学3年 すらすら英会話

Let's talk about 'Memories of Junior High School.'

Today's Point 学校生活の思い出を語り，最後に感謝の言葉を交わしましょう。

① Do you have memories of this school?

❶ Yes, I do.

② What are good memories?

❷ I have many good memories.
I enjoyed the school trip.
I also remember the music festival.
We won first place. I was glad. We
practiced singing a lot.
I remember the cooking class. Our
group made hamburger steaks, but we
burned them too much. We ate the
black hamburger steaks.

③ What is the best memory?

❸ I would say 'School trip.'

④ Tell me about your school trip.

❹ We went to Kyoto by *shinkansen*, and
I played *shogi* with my friends.
It was really a fun time.
We visited many temples. I took many
pictures. I bought souvenirs for my
family. Choosing what to buy was fun.

⑤ I was glad to study with you.
Thank you for talking with me.

❺ Thank you very much.
I also enjoyed learning with you.

⑥ Please keep in touch.

❻ Yes, I will. I'll miss you.

Useful Expressions

☐ I was glad to study with you.（あなたと一緒に勉強できて嬉しかったです）

☐ Please keep in touch.（連絡を取り合っていきましょう）

☐ I'll miss you.（あなたがいないと寂しいです）

117

hi to ku chi ei go

ひとくち英語 3

61 ⇒ 90

(61) 決めた？	(61) Have you decided it yet?
(62) まだ決まっていない。	(62) I haven't decided it yet.
(63) 実際のところ…	(63) Actually ..., / In fact,
(64) もちろん。／絶対に。	(64) Absolutely.
(65) （私は納豆が好き）一何で？	(65) (I like *natto*.) — Why?
(66) （私は納豆が好きじゃない）一何で？	(66) (I do not like *natto*.) — Why not?
(67) 言いたいことはわかります。	(67) I know what you mean.
(68) つまり…	(68) I mean ...
(69) それは面白い！	(69) That's funny!
(70) それはひどいね。	(70) That's awful. / That's terrible.
(71) 例えば？	(71) For example?
(72) お気の毒に。	(72) I'm sorry to hear that.
(73) 頑張って。	(73) Hang in there. / Good luck.
(74) それは変だね。	(74) That's strange. / That's weird.
(75) 面白そうだね。	(75) That sounds fun.
(76) うらやましいです。	(76) I envy you.
(77) （私は緊張しています）一私も。	(77) (I am nervous.) — So am I.
(78) （私はリンゴが好き）一私も。	(78) (I like *apples*.) — So do I.
(79) （私は UFO を見た）一私も。	(79) (I saw an UFO.) — So did I.
(80) どうして？	(80) How come?
(81) 何て言うのだろう？	(81) How can I say?
(82) 何て言えばいいかわかりません。	(82) I don't know what to say.
(83) どういう意味ですか？	(83) What do you mean by that?
(84) やったね！	(84) Good job! / You made it!
(85) 時と場合によります。	(85) It depends.
(86) 私の場合…	(86) In my case, ...
(87) がっかりだね。	(87) That's disappointing.
(88) もう一度言ってもらえますか？	(88) I beg your pardon?
(89) 会えないと寂しくなる。	(89) I'll miss you.
(90) これからも連絡取り合っていこうね。	(90) Let's keep in touch.

【著者紹介】

瀧沢　広人（たきざわ　ひろと）

1966年東京都東大和市に生まれる。埼玉大学教育学部小学校教員養成課程卒業後，埼玉県公立小・中学校，ベトナム日本人学校，教育委員会，中学校の教頭職を経て，現在，岐阜大学教育学部准教授として小・中学校の英語教育研究を行う。主な著書は，『中学校英語「知識＆技能」の教え方ガイド＆ワーク（3分冊）』(2024)，『板書＆展開例でよくわかる　英文法アクティビティでつくる365日の全授業　中学校外国語（3分冊）』(2023)，『中学校英語　指導スキル大全』(2022)，『目指せ！英語授業の達人40　絶対成功する！新3観点の英語テストづくり＆学習評価アイデアブック』(2021)，『同39　絶対成功する！中学校新英文法指導アイデアブック』(2021)，『同30・31・32　絶対成功する！英文法指導アイデアブック（3分冊）』(2015)，『中学校英語サポートBOOKS　話せる！書ける！英語言語活動アイデア＆ワーク66』（共著・2023），『同　苦手な子も読める！書ける！使える！中学校の英単語「超」指導法』(2021)，『授業をグーンと楽しくする英語教材シリーズ37　授業を100倍面白くする！中学校英文法パズル＆クイズ』(2014)，『同29　CanDoで英語力がめきめきアップ！　中学生のためのすらすら英文法』(2014)，『同27　文法別で入試力をぐんぐん鍛える！　中学生のための英作文ワーク』(2013)（以上，明治図書）他多数。

授業をグーンと楽しくする英語教材シリーズ49
Small Talk で使える！
トピック別・中学生のためのすらすら英会話

2024年8月初版第1刷刊　©著　者　瀧　沢　広　人
　　　　　　　　　　　　発行者　藤　原　光　政
　　　　　　　　　　　　発行所　明治図書出版株式会社
　　　　　　　　　　　　　　　　http://www.meijitosho.co.jp
　　　　　　　　　　　（企画）木山麻衣子（校正）有海有理
　　　　　　　　　　　〒114-0023　東京都北区滝野川7-46-1
　　　　　　　　　　　振替00160-5-151318　電話03(5907)6702
　　　　　　　　　　　　　　　　ご注文窓口　電話03(5907)6668
＊検印省略　　　　　　　組版所　朝日メディアインターナショナル株式会社
本書の無断コピーは，著作権・出版権にふれます。ご注意ください。
教材部分は，学校の授業過程での使用に限り，複製することができます。

Printed in Japan　　　　　　　　　　　ISBN978-4-18-398629-0
もれなくクーポンがもらえる！読者アンケートはこちらから
→

好評発売中！

毎日の英語授業の超強力サポーター！　全3巻　瀧沢広人 編著

板書＆展開例でよくわかる
英文法アクティビティでつくる
365日の全授業
中学校外国語　1年

図書番号 5731　B5判288頁・定価3,630円（10％税込）

第1章 英文法指導のポイント／第2章 365日の全授業1年【小学校の復習（場面別表現、be動詞、一般動詞、助動詞、疑問詞、命令文ほか）、3人称単数現在形、疑問詞・人称代名詞、現在進行形、不定詞（名詞的用法）、過去形、過去進行形、There is/are、感嘆文・look+形容詞】

板書＆展開例でよくわかる
英文法アクティビティでつくる
365日の全授業
中学校外国語　2年

図書番号 5732　B5判272頁・定価3,630円（10％税込）

第1章 英文法指導のポイント／第2章 365日の全授業2年【未来形、5文型（SVOO, SVOC）、接続詞、不定詞、助動詞、動名詞、疑問詞＋to不定詞、比較、受け身、既習事項の総復習】

板書＆展開例でよくわかる
英文法アクティビティでつくる
365日の全授業
中学校外国語　3年

図書番号 5733　B5判272頁・定価3,630円（10％税込）

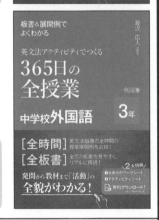

第1章 英文法指導のポイント／第2章 365日の全授業3年【現在完了形（経験用法・完了用法）、現在完了形（継続用法）・現在完了進行形、いろいろな構文、間接疑問文・SVOO（what節）、現在分詞・過去分詞、関係代名詞、仮定法、既習事項の総復習、付録［知識・技能］確認プリント】

明治図書　携帯・スマートフォンからは **明治図書ONLINEへ** 書籍の検索、注文ができます。▶▶▶

http://www.meijitosho.co.jp ＊併記4桁の図書番号（英数字）でHP、携帯での検索・注文が簡単に行えます。

〒114-0023　東京都北区滝野川7-46-1　ご注文窓口　TEL (03)5907-6668　FAX (050)3156-2790